T0318033

An Unhurried Leader

THE LASTING FRUIT
OF DAILY INFLUENCE

Alan Fadling

IVP Books

An imprint of InterVarsity Press
Downers Grove, Illinois

InterVarsity Press
P.O. Box 1400, Downers Grove, IL 60515-1426
ivpress.com
email@ivpress.com

©2017 by Alan Fadling

All rights reserved. No part of this book may be reproduced in any form without written permission from InterVarsity Press.

InterVarsity Press® is the book-publishing division of InterVarsity Christian Fellowship/USA®, a movement of students and faculty active on campus at hundreds of universities, colleges, and schools of nursing in the United States of America, and a member movement of the International Fellowship of Evangelical Students. For information about local and regional activities, visit intervarsity.org.

All Scripture quotations, unless otherwise indicated, are taken from THE HOLY BIBLE, NEW INTERNATIONAL VERSION®, NIV® Copyright © 1973, 1978, 1984, 2011 by Biblica, Inc.™ Used by permission. All rights reserved worldwide.

While any stories in this book are true, some names and identifying information may have been changed to protect the privacy of individuals.

Cover design: Cindy Kiple
Interior design: Jeanna Wiggins
Images: Ocean storm: © andrej67/iStockphoto
Raindrops: © gaiamoments/iStockphoto
Window and sailboats: © Sandra Cunningham / Trevillion Images
Paper sailboat: © Dokmaihaeng / iStockphoto

ISBN 978-0-8308-4631-3 (paperback)
ISBN 978-0-8308-4634-4 (hardcover)
ISBN 978-0-8308-9091-0 (digital)

Printed in the United States of America ♾

 As a member of the Green Press Initiative, InterVarsity Press is committed to protecting the environment and to the responsible use of natural resources. To learn more, visit greenpressinitiative.org.

Library of Congress Cataloging-in-Publication Data

Names: Fadling, Alan, 1961- author.
Title: An unhurried leader : the lasting fruit of daily influence / Alan
Fadling.
Description: Downers Grove : InterVarsity Press, 2017. | Includes
bibliographical references.
Identifiers: LCCN 2017004999 (print) | LCCN 2017012806 (ebook) | ISBN
9780830890910 (eBook) | ISBN 9780830846344 (hardcover : alk. paper)
Subjects: LCSH: Leadership—Religious aspects—Christianity.
Classification: LCC BV4597.53.L43 (ebook) | LCC BV4597.53.L43 F33 2017
(print) | DDC 253—dc23
LC record available at https://lccn.loc.gov/2017004999

P   21   20   19   18   17   16   15   14   13   12   11   10   9   8   7   6   5   4   3   2

Y   34   33   32   31   30   29   28   27   26   25   24   23

"As my own leadership responsibilities have significantly increased in recent years, I can only say 'many thanks!' to Alan for offering such a timely, rooted, and integrated vision of the very real possibilities that exist for leaders who choose an unhurried life. It's all true! And it's an ongoing pursuit, which is why his book is so helpful. Rich with practical examples of practices to support this way of life and leadership, *An Unhurried Leader* is a great guide for anyone who seeks to lead from a place of overflow rather than deficit."

Mindy Caliguire, founder, Soul Care

"In *An Unhurried Leader*, Fadling uses the Bible to unpack the wisdom of choosing to be led by Jesus as we lead others, so that our pace, ways, and results align with God's will. This is a book I highly recommend to everyone who is intentional about joining God at work and working God's way."

Jean Paul Ndagijimana, corporate chaplain, Lift Up Limited, Rwanda

"At the heart of Christian spirituality is love. Jesus instructed us to love God and our neighbor. Paul said the greatest virtue is love. But love takes time— and time is the one thing a hurried leader does not have. The results of unloving, anxious, fear-based Christian leadership are now all around us, as seen in the culture-wide rejection of church. In *An Unhurried Leader*, Alan Fadling points the way out of hurried leadership that kills the souls of leaders. He reveals leadership steeped in spiritual abundance and joy. This is not a how-to book. This book lays out a path to becoming a better sort of person, who is then naturally a better kind of leader."

Todd Hunter, Anglican bishop, author of *Our Character at Work*

"Alan set out to offer an inspiring vision of leadership that is less hurried and more fruitful, less hectic and more joyful—and that he did. With the biblical text as his consistent backdrop, each principle, practice, and suggested reflection creates a unique mosaic for every spiritual leader desirous of living an abundant life."

Stephen A. Macchia, founder and president of Leadership Transformations, author of *Becoming a Healthy Church*, *Crafting a Rule of Life*, and *Broken and Whole*

"This book works! I began reading it hurriedly, but its soothing, consistent truth drew me to slow down and sense the presence of God."

Jan Johnson, speaker, author of *Abundant Simplicity* and *Meeting God in Scripture*

"Alan Fadling has done it again! He writes in a way that challenges me to rethink my leadership. I love him and hate him at the same time for reminding me to love from an overflow and abundance rather than leading on empty. He doesn't just describe the problem, instead in *An Unhurried Leader* he gently and graciously guides the reader toward change that is doable and a reflection of the genius of Jesus' unhurried way of living and leading. Another must read!"

Doug Fields, author of *Your First Two Years in Youth Ministry*

TO CHUCK MILLER
(1935-2017)

With gratitude to my friend, my brother,

a spiritual father and mentor

in the ways of Christlike leadership.

Contents

ONE

Becoming an Unhurried Leader

As I began writing this book, I decided that taking un-hurried opportunities to write might help me capture the spirit of what I want to communicate. I've long enjoyed road cycling as a way of getting some exercise and—maybe more important—of slowing from 65 mph to 15 or 20 mph, outside and in. So I packed a couple of cycle bags and left the house on my bicycle with my computer and a few changes of clothing. I rode to the nearest train station, took a train south to the coastal California town of Carlsbad and booked a couple of nights in a hotel room. As I traveled, I felt that familiar inner drivenness fueled by the false formula that busyness equates to productivity. I know slowing down inside is crucial to spiritual health and productive leadership, but slowing down remains a difficult spiritual discipline for me.

On my way south, I realized that both my dependence on train schedules and the limitations of cycling versus driving exposed the reality of just how little control I actually have in this world. Still, this little trip was one of many ways to become a more unhurried leader.

I want to be unhurried enough to discern God's voice and sense his guidance for my life, my relationships, and my writing. When my heart is a hamster wheel, my inner life becomes a blur.

My train route takes me south along the Pacific Ocean. I find that even a glimpse of the ocean helps my soul rest. There is something about the blue horizon that reminds me of God's immensity and just how spacious his love for me is. The ocean unhurries my soul.

The truth is that whatever progress I'm making, I continue to wrestle with my addiction to drivenness and anxious activity, and I expect I will struggle with this addiction to some degree for the rest of my life. I also expect the most challenging aspects of this journey will involve my roles and relationships of influence.

I'm a parent to three young adult sons. I'm a spiritual mentor to leaders. I'm the founder of a new nonprofit. And in these roles and relationships, I'm often tempted to frantically rush to take control of situations in hopes of making good things happen. That kind of unholy hurry may make me look busy, but too often it keeps me from actually being fruitful in the ways Jesus wants me to be.

Jesus modeled grace-paced leadership. To learn from him, we begin not with leading but with following.

LEADERS AS FOLLOWERS

So what kind of book is this? A how-to book with simple-but-not-easy, clearly defined steps to leadership success? I've learned much from such books, but that's not the book I have written. Do books like these give me insight I can put into practice? Of course. Do they offer wisdom for all of us? Certainly. But this book is something different.

In these pages I hope to offer an inspiring vision of leadership that is less hurried and more fruitful, less hectic and more joyful. I will provide practical insights I've learned along the way to help you make your way fruitfully into all the unhurried leadership opportunities God has for you. I hope you'll discover with me that an unhurried leader grows ever more confident that all the truth and all the wisdom we need is available to us in Jesus (1 Cor 1:30). There is no kingdom-fruitful wisdom apart from him.

Jesus sets the pace of my following, and I'm not trying to be super spiritual here. This is just basic kingdom reality: I cannot lead for the good or the honor of God's kingdom if I am not seeking his kingdom first and foremost in my life *and* my work. Otherwise, I end up promoting my own little kingdom agendas, all the while assuming I am doing so in the name of Jesus. It happens all the time. It's happened far too frequently in my own leadership.

Too often I've lived and led fueled by the idea that the one who hurries gets the most done for God. This is so different from the spiritual wisdom that the one who hurries delays the things of God. What I've been discovering is that unhurried leadership is actually more fruitful *because* it is more unhurried, not *in spite of* that slower pace. My mentoring of others, for example, is among the most unhurried ways to have lasting kingdom influence. There are no instant strategies to becoming a faithful disciple. Just like anything relational, such influence takes time—years or even decades. In this book, I'll share what I've been learning in my unhurried journey as a disciple of Jesus. After all, kingdom leadership is rooted in followership. I'll share from God-given successes and all-too-familiar personal stumbles along the way.

HAVING A HOLY INFLUENCE

When I talk about leadership in this book, I'm not limiting that to people like CEOs and senior pastors who have a wide span of organizational responsibility. I certainly hope that what I have to say will be a significant help to fellow organizational leaders. But I'm writing not just about organizational leadership. I'm writing about life leadership. I'm talking about spiritual influence, about kingdom of God influence. Each of us has been planted in particular places among particular people whom we might bless and benefit by sharing something good we're receiving from God's good kingdom.

We all have some scope of influence in the lives of others. We need not have a *position* of influence to be a *person* of influence. Many influential people in my life over the years had no position of organizational authority in my life, but the way they lived and worked inspired and motivated me to a better way of living and leading.

I would love for us to learn together how to live as blessed members of God's good kingdom who can share with others from his abundance in our lives. What a beautiful impact we would have on our world. We could grow in our trust of God's grace shown us in Jesus so that our lives actually become like an ever-expanding river of not only his grace but also his goodness and generosity. God might fill our lives with more of his love and compassion than we can contain so we can share that "more" with others. Our influence would be the overflow of God's very presence filling us and spilling from our lives in ways that bring refreshment, encouragement, and holy energy to others.

What if each of us lived this way? Imagine the changes that might come to our little place in the world! Wouldn't this be significant, even life-changing leadership influence? What if parents found the roots of their life sunk deep into the infinitely vast love of their heavenly Father, so much so that their parenting was simply the expression of that abundant divine love? What if men and women in business found in God inspiration for a creative, powerful, and unselfish vision of their work? What a profound impact they would have on their fellow workers and clients! So I'm speaking to anyone with an inner hunger to have a holy influence in this world. Where our lives touch the lives of others, may we enrich them rather than diminish them, may we generously give and not selfishly expect something from them.

Our influence will grow as we cultivate a way of living and working that feels far less draining over time and far more energized by the Spirit to the point of overflowing. We will experience more and more moments when we feel as if we are living and leading from abundance rather than out of sheer willpower or our own detached-from-God human efforts.

Let's learn together how to more closely follow Jesus in his way of being open to the people the Father brought across his path. Let's learn how to put down our agendas and welcome divine surprises that weren't on our calendars or to-do lists. Let's learn to stop labeling as interruptions to our work what may actually be God-given opportunities to do his good work in that moment. Let's learn to make good plans rooted in our fellowship with God, but may we hold those plans loosely enough for him to guide us when we implement them. Jesus has invited us into this reality of an ongoing conversational relationship with God. I love this way of living and leading.

SPIRITUAL LEADERSHIP

One of the ways inner hurry has hampered my leadership is when I've rushed to the conclusion that I am not a leader because I am not like a leader I admire. That person seems more like the ideal leader I imagine I'm not. But many leaders like me are more like Timothy than Peter: more tempted by fear than by pride, more likely to be self-deprecating than self-promoting. Unhurried leadership operates from a peaceful confidence that God has made me, that God is remaking me, and that God has invited me to live a life of influence from that very place and as that very person. God is making me to be the person of influence *I* was meant to be.

Some people might want to call being an unhurried leader "spiritual leadership." There's truth there, but I would use that phrase with a bit of caution. Some will hear *spiritual* as meaning somehow detached from a real life of parenting, earning a living, paying our bills, mowing the lawn, and such. I use *spiritual,* however, to describe the most essential inner reality of who we are. Therefore, I don't limit spiritual leadership to a leader's prayer life, moral character, or religious observances. Spiritual leadership is leadership rooted in the deepest reality there is: living in vital relationship with God through Jesus, and then bearing the good fruit of that communion.

Furthermore, the term *spiritual leadership* can help us remember that while what leaders *do* matters immensely, who leaders *are* matters even more. Of course what leaders do matters, but we sometimes overestimate the impact of things we leaders do and pay insufficient attention to the impact of who we are becoming. And who we are is the substance that fuels our actions. What kind of person is doing the things we are doing? Are we becoming more generous, more others-concerned, or more patient? How might such a person do the same work differently than a person who is fine with remaining self-seeking, self-promoting, or impatient? Two people can do the very same thing with very different outcomes. The same task gets done, but the resulting fruit can be radically different.

I recently had lunch with a pastor of a church located in downtown Los Angeles. We talked about how too many people with a leadership title see their roles as something they must manage on their own *for* God, rather than being a means by which, *with* God, they might be a blessing to the people around them. The result is often anxiety, self-importance, fear, or self-promotion, the kind of fruit that bears no aroma of God's glorious and inviting presence. Spiritual leadership is not so much about managing something for God as much as it is expressing the life of God in the unique situation we find ourselves in. What if our leadership influence were more about overflow than about managing what we perceive to be the limited, if not meager, resources at our disposal? What if God's kingdom really has come and I'm actually invited to be a key player in people's vision and knowledge of their Creator?

THE PURPOSES OF GOD

So this spiritual—this unhurried—leadership is a process of learning to work in harmony with the purposes of God. It is also the awareness that so much of what God does begins in people's hearts. How can we as unhurried leaders be involved in this aspect of God's work? One way is to join Jesus and the Spirit in prayer. Jesus is never too busy to talk to the Father about our good. Are we too busy to seek the Father for the good of our spouses, our children, our friends, our neighbors, or our coworkers? If so, I'd say we're too busy.

Hurried leadership makes me think of a childhood toy called a Chinese finger trap. This long, narrow cylinder is often woven from bamboo strips. A child puts a finger from one hand into one end and a finger from the other hand in the other end and pulls. The trap tightens on each of the child's fingers. Without thinking, the child's instinct to get out of the trap is to pull harder. But the harder he pulls, the tighter the trap becomes. The child needs to do the opposite of what he assumes is right and instead push his fingers toward each other. Doing so will loosen the trap enough to extricate his little digits.

When we get into hurried, anxious places in our lives, how do we respond? Do we, like a child first experiencing a finger trap, try harder and go faster only to find that life gets even more hurried, worried, and cramped? What if we learned to do exactly the opposite of what we would do impulsively? We might experience what Isaiah described: "In repentance and rest is your salvation, in quietness and trust is your strength" (Is 30:15).

I've found those words from Isaiah especially helpful whenever I think about having a more unhurried approach to my leadership relationships and roles. To be specific, I see salvation and strength as leadership categories. Throughout Scripture, God's people seek human leaders like judges or kings who will be strong on their behalf and get them out of the messes in which they find themselves. It's not much different today. But, through Isaiah, God paints a very different picture of what true salvation and strength look like.

When we look for someone who will save us from our troubles, the qualifications at the top of the list are rarely repentance and rest. We tend to want leaders who will take charge and get moving. Repentance sounds, to the untrained ear, like a reversal or perhaps like a lack of confidence. And as for rest? We want leaders who are going to work until they solve our problem—or drop trying. And when we think of strong leaders, we don't tend to look for someone who would best be described by the words *quiet* and *trusting*. At least in North America, we often seem to be drawn to bombastic, self-assured leaders who seem to know what they're doing—and we hope like crazy they'll get something, the right thing, done. But Isaiah said that we'll find salvation—help, wholeness, or rescue—in repentance and rest. He said that we'll find strength—power, influence, and energy—in quietness and trust. Unhurried leaders are different.

- Rather than fill their lives with noise, unhurried leaders make time for silence in which to listen (quietness).

- Rather than allow anxiety to drive them, unhurried leaders learn to depend on a reliable God who invites them to join a good kingdom work already well underway (trust).

- Rather than tackle self-initiated projects under the guise of doing them *for* God, unhurried leaders humbly orient themselves to the Leader of all, learning to take their cues from him (repentance).

- Unhurried leaders also learn to rest as hard as they work.

- Rather than measuring the productivity of their lives only in terms of what they *do*, unhurried leaders understand the importance of certain things they *don't* do.

Quietness, trust, repentance, and *rest* are words that speak, at least in part, to those things. So what was Israel's response to God's invitation to repentance, rest, quietness, and trust? Isaiah described it:

> But you would have none of it.
> You said, "No, we will flee on horses."
> Therefore, you will flee!

You said, "We will ride off on swift horses."
Therefore your pursuers will be swift! (Isaiah 30:15-16)

Unfortunately, Israel answered God with an unqualified no. Specifically, they said, "No, we will flee on horses." They decided to rely on horsepower. To try harder. Do more. Work longer. Hard work and effort are good, God-given capacities, but when these become separated from a living communion with God, they can become destructive rather than constructive. We can find ourselves running past God rather than walking with God. And, unfortunately, Israel would use horsepower to run away rather than engage or confront their enemies in the strength of God. And, sadly, if horsepower didn't do the job, they said they would opt for *more* horsepower—not just horses but *swift* horses. In this case, Israel's more horsepower was met with their enemy's more horsepower ("Therefore your pursuers will be swift!"). Doesn't it sound a lot like that child's finger trap game, only with greater consequences?

When I have resisted relating to God and life on the basis of trust and humble respect, I've usually chosen the path of horsepower. When that doesn't work, I've often upped the ante, choosing more horsepower. But those hurried, high horsepower ways of living and working leave me dogged by enemies that have even more horsepower than I do.

Practically speaking, when I wake up to being in horsepower-only mode, I feel angry, or anxious, or drained. In such moments, I seek to take even a few minutes to be quiet and still, to allow my heart and mind to remember that God is with me. When anxious thoughts start to invade and rule that moment of silence, I allow myself to gently remember God's gracious invitation: "Turn to face me. Relax in me. Let me quiet your heart. Trust me." Then I remember that I'm not doing this work alone or for a God who is distant or disengaged. I let myself remember that I'm doing this work because of God's invitation and in his loving and empowering presence. When I take this kind of break, I often find that a fresh sense of the salvation and strength Isaiah described becomes the context of my thoughts, emotions, and intentions as I move forward. I experience the fruit of the beautiful prayer Paul prayed for his friends in Thessalonica: "May our Lord Jesus Christ himself and God our Father, who loved us and by his grace gave us eternal encouragement and good hope, encourage your hearts and strengthen you in every good deed and word" (2 Thess 2:16-17).

LEADERSHIP: SELF-SERVICE OR SERVING OTHERS?

In my own leadership journey, I've found that a critical question I need to ask myself often is "What am I seeking?" How I answer that question determines whether or not my approach to leadership is healthy and sustainable. If I am truly seeking first the loving reign of God and God's ways in my life and, through me, in ministry, then—in the spirit of Jesus' words in the Sermon on the Mount—I find that I have everything I need. Jesus says that "all these things will be given to you as well" (Mt 6:33). While he may be talking there about basic physical needs, I believe the application extends to whatever it is we might truly need in order to lead well.

When I seek God's kingdom first, I find that my vision of leadership is rooted in the abundance of God's presence; no longer am I adrift in experiences of apparent scarcity. Leading from a place of perceived scarcity can make me resentful, fearful, anxious, and controlling. Leading from a place of real abundance enables me to do so from a place of joy, peace, and security. I begin to find myself in trouble when my leadership becomes an attempt to find satisfaction for an empty soul rather than being a place where I can serve from a God-filled soul. My leadership has sometimes been a frantic attempt to establish some sense of an identity I feel I don't yet possess. I'm seeking a God-honoring way of leading that is fueled by a secure sense of the value and identity I have in him. But I've too often found myself leading from a place of unholy dissatisfaction rather than from a place of holy satisfaction.

In the past and especially at my low moments, my leadership efforts were basically my search for something to fill me. It was my anxiety hurrying toward some sense of control. It was my recognition deficit racing around, looking for someone to like something I've done or said. It was my self-doubt looking for some sort of outside reinforcement. What I'm grateful for is that, more recently and in my better moments, I'm discovering that leadership can be fullness looking for places to overflow. When I serve and lead from a place of being relaxed instead of anxious, I serve with far more creativity, compassion, and confidence. When I serve and lead confident in God's love for me, I don't need those I'm serving to say, "Well done!" I'm already living in God's affirmation and encouragement. I can welcome the affirming words others might speak as a free gift to me rather than something I desperately need.

I think of the words Jesus called out as he stood in the temple courts on the last day of a Jewish festival: "Anyone thirsty? If you are, come to me. Trust me and your soul will become a place from which rivers of living water flow" (Jn 7:37-39, my paraphrase). I see overflow from that river of living water as a metaphor for what I want to have happening in my leadership and ministry. What I bring to Jesus as a thirst can be transformed into more refreshment and life than I can possibly hold. That abundance, that excess, that overflow can become manifest in my work, my service, my leadership.

So unhurried leadership is *overflow leadership*—a term that always feels so pregnant and powerful. There is always an overwhelming and affirming response when I share this vision with fellow leaders. We all recognize the difference between leading from empty or leading from overflow. Our hurried approaches to influence usually find us functioning in the former category.

RATHER THAN . . . INSTEAD OF . . .

As a leader, rather than acting like a needy person trying to get something from those I lead, I am invited to work like a generous and gracious servant. Rather than trying to prove something about myself, I can lead as an expression of something already God-established. Rather than leading in order to compensate for some sense of personal deficiency, I lead to communicate and share a fullness I already have. Patience, gentleness, kindness, and compassion are all expressions of that God-given fullness. Anxiety, anger, harshness, and selfish ambition are indications of my emptiness.

Rather than bringing my thirsts to my leadership roles and activities, rather than seeking something there to quench those thirsts, I can bring my thirsts to Jesus and find in him a river of living water. And in addition to satisfying my desperate thirsts, that living water can flow through me to bring the life, refreshment, and encouragement that people need in those places where I serve as a leader.

Instead of bringing my thirst for affirmation or recognition to my leadership roles and relationships of influence, seeking some positive response from those I lead, I bring this thirst to Jesus. I hear from him the same words he heard from his Father, "You are my beloved son. I'm so pleased with you" (see Mt 3:17). From this place of knowing the Father's deep affection, I can bring an abundance of affirmation to those I serve rather than seeking affirmation from them. What a difference that makes!

Instead of bringing my thirst for security to my work, I bring this thirst to Jesus. I can then find in him the security I long for, and I can minister from security rather than for security. Rather than making the futile attempt to control people and situations in order to achieve a false sense of security, I can lead with confidence and peace because I have a deep sense of safety and a solid trust in God's provision for me.

So, for example, when I stand to speak to a group, I sometimes feel anxious and self-conscious at first. If I stay in that place, I won't speak with much freedom or creative energy. But if I can relax, if I can remember that I am not there to speak on my own behalf but on behalf of Another, and if I can trust that what this group needs will be available to me to share with them, then I experience—by God's grace—a simple flow of good things to speak. I rest, knowing that what I need God has already given me. It reminds me of Jesus' promise to his followers who would find themselves in a much more serious situation: "When they arrest you, do not worry about what to say or how to say it. At that time you will be given what to say, for it will not be you speaking, but the Spirit of your Father speaking through you" (Mt 10:19-20).

So, positive expressions of leadership as overflow are not dependent on a favorable situation that easily gives rise to peace and joy. And I'm not talking about an emotional buoyancy or a good mood rooted in pleasant and preferred surroundings. I'm speaking of leadership that overflows from deeper places of confidence, joy, peace, and courage, from subterranean places of holy trust in God. Our fullness of peace even in a worrisome season, or our fullness of joy even when we're in a long, dark valley, or our fullness of love even when events seem to call into question the current level of God's care—the overflow from fullness like this results in rich, heartfelt ministry that is good for those being served and that glorifies God.

LOOKING AHEAD

Let me give you a little look ahead at this vision of unhurried leadership as an expression of overflow. In the spirit of the counsel John Ortberg once received from a mentor ("You must ruthlessly eliminate hurry from your life"), we must also eliminate hurry from our leadership. We hurry when we think that the first thing to be done as a leader is "do something." Of course there is action to be taken in leadership. We must not allow fear, procrastination, or laziness to hinder fruitful activity. But often the first thing to be done as a leader is something more receptive than active, something like listening, seeing, or reflecting. I've done too many things that didn't matter very much because I felt I had to do *something*.

And in case you think I'm writing this leadership book from a place of ease, I want you to know that much of the first draft was written in a season when I made one of the biggest leadership decisions of my adult life. I stepped away from what felt like a familiar and safe place with good friends, a place where I'd served on staff for eighteen years, to launch a new nonprofit called Unhurried Living. I stepped away from certainty into uncertainty, away from security to insecurity. The temptation to rush into quick solutions and instant answers was great. But living in this place of new beginnings with an unhurried orientation has already been more fruitful than I could have hoped.

At the end of each chapter, you will find a practice in unhurried leadership that I invite you to try out as well as some questions for personal reflection or group discussion. I'm so glad to have you join me in this journey. It's so good to live and lead this way together.

PRACTICE: *LEARNING TO BREATHE*

Just as the Chinese finger trap offers me a metaphor of unhurried living, breathing offers another metaphor that has helped me think about healthy rhythms of spiritual life and leadership. In terms of this metaphor, at times my way of life and leadership has looked like I was trying only to exhale. Output. Doing. Extension of effort. But breathing only works if we inhale as well as exhale. Besides, I don't have anything to exhale if I haven't breathed in first. So holy influence is not merely about my activities; it is also about my receptivities. Holy influence is about both what I do and who I am becoming.

Give this a try: exhale, but then don't inhale right away. After a couple of seconds, try exhaling without inhaling again. Then try exhaling once more. It just doesn't work. Take a nice, deep, re-freshing breath. Doesn't that feel good?

As a way of praying this way, you could try an inhale and exhale approach to the day ahead of you. Exhale and mention to God some appointment, task, meeting, or work that you expect to engage that day. Then inhale something of who God is and what God gives that would bless you and those you might be with later. "[Exhale] I think of my lunch appointment today with John. [Inhale] Thank you for the good words you'll give me to bless him. [Exhale] Thanks for the op-portunity that we'll talk about. [Inhale] I welcome your creativity, your peace, your holy curiosity in our time together," and so on. Try to breathe slowly and evenly. Let it be a way of becoming still and re-membering that God really is God (Ps 46:10 paraphrased).

Unhurried Leadership Reflections

1. In this chapter, we talked about a number of internal factors—like anxiety, anger, or insecurity—that can rev us up in our roles and relationships. What inner dynamics do you believe contribute to your hurry? When might you have an honest conversation with God about how you can stand strong against those dynamics and actually slow down?

2. What thoughts and feelings do you have as you begin reading this book about unhurried leadership? In what ways does the idea of unhurried leadership attract you? In what ways do you feel re-sistant or uncertain? Explain why.

3. We talked about leadership that learns how to "seek first God's kingdom and God's right way." Other than the initial seeking that led to your salvation, what are you sometimes tempted to seek first or put first *instead* of God's person, God's presence, God's prior-ities? What might it look like in those very situations to truly begin to seek God first instead?

4. You read about the idea of leadership as overflow seeking opportunities to bless versus leadership as a thirst seeking satisfaction from achievements or the affirmation of others. In what ways do you identify with each of these two very different approaches to leadership? When and where do you tend to bring your thirsts to your work? Prayerfully consider what leadership might actually look like and how you might be blessed if you were to bring those particular thirsts to Jesus. Imagine what those thirsts would look like if God transformed them into springs of living water.

TWO

Leading from Abundance

A FEW YEARS AGO, MY WIFE, GEM, AND I joined a tour group that visited Israel and Jordan. One of the most remarkable experiences we had was at the Dead Sea. When they call it *dead*, they aren't kidding. No plants on the shore. No evidence of life in the water. Nothing.

The experience brought to mind a passage—Ezekiel 47—that has been a meaningful metaphor in my life and leadership for many years. In this chapter God gave the prophet Ezekiel a vision of a future temple out of which flows an ever-expanding river that renews the desert and brings life to the Dead Sea. The temple itself is the place of God's presence, where his people acknowledge him and worship him, where we offer our gifts and our very selves. And the temple is the source of everything that happens in this vision. The river that flows out from the temple is living water, increasing as it moves away from the temple. The river flows on out through the wilderness into the Dead Sea and heals what is broken, refreshes what is dry and weary, nourishes what is hungry, and brings life to what is dead. What a beautiful vision of unhurried leadership! Unhurried leadership always has time for the temple.

BECOMING A TEMPLE

Central in this vision of blessing is a temple from which water begins to flow as a trickle (Ezek 47:1-2). Earlier in the book of Ezekiel, the man who showed this vision to the prophet had shown him the empty temple being filled with God's presence: "The glory of the LORD entered the temple through the gate facing east. Then the Spirit lifted me up and brought me into the inner court, and the glory of the LORD filled the temple" (Ezek 43:4-5). God became gloriously present! And how do the servants of the temple respond to this presence? A few chapters earlier, Ezekiel mentions that the sons of Zadok were the only Levites allowed to "draw near to the LORD to minister before him" (Ezek 40:46). This is a potent statement about our primary work in kingdom leadership.

A number of years ago I had the opportunity to have lunch with a monk who was in his nineties. I asked him about his ministry at the monastery. I wondered what roles or tasks he was responsible for at his advanced age. When I said, "What is your main ministry here at the monastery?" I was expecting some job title or list of tasks. The monk's answer? "God." One word. He didn't tell me about any monastery jobs he did. He understood his primary ministry as not so much *for* God but *to* God. His life was rooted in God.

What if we thought about our work and our responsibilities as a ministry to God? We could choose to regard our relationships, our opportunities, and our responsibilities as places through which God's living water flows from him through us to others. Like this monk, we can choose to see that our first work is not what we do for others but what we do with God. We draw near to minister to God, and we live our lives and lead God's people from this abundant and glorious place of communion with him.

When I think about people whose lives have influenced me, of course I remember things they've done for me or said to me. But often I remember even more clearly something about the kind of person each of these men and women has been with me. Let me share with you an example.

Many years ago I served as college pastor in a large evangelical church, and one of my responsibilities was overseeing the church's ministry efforts through missionaries we financially supported. We traditionally had an annual fall missions conference, and the opportunity opened up to have one of my heroes speak. J. Oswald Sanders—author of *Spiritual Leadership*, a book many of my fellow pastors greatly admired—would be in town on the weekend of our missions conference, and he had no commitments. Now, many decades later, I can't remember much of what Sanders said, but I still remember the depth, gentleness, grace, and kindness of his manner. There was a deep-rootedness about his life, and the presence of God with him was unmistakable.

At one point during the week, Dr. Sanders needed someone to give him a ride to meet with a friend who was about an hour away from our church. I was unavailable, so my intern had the opportunity to spend an uninterrupted hour in the car with him. He couldn't wait to talk with this seasoned saint who, from our perspective, had written *the* book on spiritual leadership. This young man, just starting out in ministry, asked a question perhaps any of us might have asked in such a situation: "What is the secret of spiritual leadership?"

Without missing a beat, Dr. Sanders answered the question with one word: "God." That's all he said. He had learned in nearly ninety years of life that the secret of growing in godliness is God. The secret of my spiritual leadership is God. And I learn to enter into the power God offers us as I live in more deeply rooted communion with God through my friendship with Jesus and the Spirit's power.

When I shared this story with my wife, she responded, "When will I learn that God really is the answer to everything?" When indeed?

Both the monk I met and Dr. Sanders lived out this simple yet profound sense of God being the center of life and the source of effective leadership. These real-life examples seem key to understanding the words of Jesus: "Seek first [God's] kingdom and his righteousness, and all these things [food, clothes, basic needs] will be given to you as well" (Mt 6:33). I find this simple but not easy instruction to be an effective approach to leadership. We will experience grace in our lives as well as our leadership efforts when our first seeking remains the reign of God in us and through us. I'm talking about a following-Jesus way of life and leadership by which God makes us more like his Son. We become, like Jesus, people who increasingly say the words the Father is saying or do the works the Father is doing or assess situations as the Father discerns. Our life and leadership become a growing expression of divine overflow.

A PLACE OF GOD'S GLORIOUS PRESENCE

Ezekiel 47 shows us a river of living water flowing from the temple that brings life wherever it goes because its very source is the presence of God in the temple. God is not specifically mentioned in this vision, but he is essential to the scene, just as Emmanuel—"God is with us"—is essential to living a God-honoring life on this earth.

But how often I forget the practical reality of God with me in Jesus! And how often the presence of trouble, or anxiety, or fear, or anger becomes more real to me than God's presence. Instead of resting in the Presence, I too often wrestle with the presence of negative thoughts and emotions. I let myself become distracted instead of staying focused on God.

One of my great needs is not just remembering and acknowledging the reality of God always being with me, but remembering just who this God really is. So many distorted images of God exist in my mind and heart, resulting in a perspective on the Almighty that repels me rather than draws me in. God isn't a human father having a bad day or a boss or supervisor who can never quite be pleased. And God isn't a cold and judgmental authority I have to cower before. The God whom Jesus shows me is a good Father. God wants the best for me. God loves with a love far sweeter than any human love. God finds pleasure in me when I am not much of a pleasure even to myself. And God doesn't have bad days.

Highlighting this temple reality are David's words of prayer in Psalm 27:4:

> One thing I ask from the LORD,
>   this only do I seek:
> that I may dwell in the house of the LORD
>   all the days of my life,
> to gaze on the beauty of the LORD
>   and to seek him in his temple.

David wanted to always be at home in the presence of God. The temple itself was beautiful in both design and reality, but its beauty paled next to the breathtaking beauty of the God who dwelt there, a divine beauty that inspired heartfelt worship. Too often I have reduced worship to singing songs with other God-followers when we gather for church. Worship is a life lived in honor of my loving Father in heaven. It is an unselfconscious life rooted in, fixed on, and nourished by God. Unhurried leadership flows from going before God with a singleness of purpose and childlike simplicity. This is one way to understand the idea of holiness. *Holiness* is a vocabulary word from the temple.

What then flows naturally out of worship is offering. Ezekiel saw the beginning of the flow of this river "coming down from under the south side of the temple, south of the altar" (Ezek 47:1). An altar is a place of offering and sacrifices, and it makes complete sense that this river begins at the altar. Life flows from places where we fully offer ourselves to whatever God wishes to do in or through us. Living water flows when loving surrender is our response to sacrificial love. Such an offering or sacrifice is not a *should*. This offering is a heartfelt response to God's very real, very present love and commitment to us as evidenced in Christ. This connection between worship and offering has provided me a new awareness of both who God is and the significance of his invitation to me. In turn, this awareness draws me to a new or deeper response of offering myself to him. We say a little no to our own will so that we might say a heartier yes to God's.

As Paul pointed out to the Christians at Corinth, our bodies are a place where God dwells, a temple (1 Cor 6:19-20). The body of Christ—the people of God living in loving and fruitful relationship with one another—is a place from which the life and vitality of God might so fill us to overflowing that we become a means of God's blessing and goodness in our world.

BECOMING A RIVER

Bernard of Clairvaux, a twelfth-century reformer in the Benedictine order of monks, offered this insight into life and leadership as overflow:

> The [one] who is wise, therefore, will see [their] life as more like a reservoir than a canal. The canal simultaneously pours out what it receives; the reservoir retains the water till it is filled, then [offers] the overflow without loss to itself. . . . Today there are many in the Church who act like canals; the reservoirs are far too rare. . . . They want to pour [this stream] forth before they have been filled; they are more ready to speak than to listen, impatient to teach what they have not grasped, and full of presumption to govern others while they know not how to govern themselves.

Nearly nine hundred years after Bernard, we don't seem much different. Bernard's metaphor complements the Ezekiel 47 language: the temple is a reservoir—a place of fullness—and the river is a canal, a place of flow.

As the man went eastward with a measuring line in his hand, he measured off a thousand cubits and then led me through water that was ankle-deep. He measured off another thousand cubits and led me through water that was knee-deep. He measured off another thousand and led me through water that was up to the waist. He measured off another thousand, but now it was a river that I could not cross, because the water had risen and was deep enough to swim in—a river that no one could cross. (Ezek 47:3-5)

Hurried leaders are quick to do and slow to be; quick to speak but slow to listen; quick to teach and slow to learn; quick to lead others but slow to let God lead them beside his still waters.

Too often I have been a hurried leader. In my roles and relationships of influence, I find within me the desire to try to control my circumstances and the lives of others. But in my personal journey of spiritual growth and leadership development, I have come to see just how little control I have over circumstances and decisions others will make, whether my own family, people with whom I work, or individuals I serve in my vocational efforts. Yet this vision of a river of living water that flows from the temple has deepened my conviction that something vital and transformative is already happening and that I'm invited to join in its flow. My work can be a joining in the flow of what God is already doing to bring new life, vitality, fruitfulness, and renewal to the world.

When it comes to our strategy for having a godly influence on others, we seem to have the choice of making a splash or joining the Lord's flow. What do I mean by this? It's easy to have a short-range view of the impact of my life. Making a splash would mean doing something dramatic and easily measured in the near term. Joining the flow of what the Lord is already doing requires a longer-range perspective and the recognition that change that lasts rarely happens quickly. The kind of flow pictured in Ezekiel 47 may begin as an un-impressive trickle, but it can grow into a mighty river. Too often we start big but end small. What about a strategy that starts small and grows over time? And what about my learning to live out my life as one at home in the temple? I must keep the channel clear so that God's life, love, joy, and peace might flow freely through me for the benefit of those around me.

Starting at the temple—being filled to overflowing with God's love and power, not moving until he says so—doesn't always mean imme-diate results. In fact, even with that vital starting point, what flows out from my life of worship and abiding in Christ may seem even less than a trickle. But patience will see that less than a trickle gradually grows into a river that cannot be crossed.

I am impressed by the sequence of this vision. The man led Ezekiel through water that became progressively deeper until they reached a point where the river was, so to speak, beyond Ezekiel's depth. I would prefer to remain where the river feels manageable rather than continue my journey to places that overwhelm me. But only when the river has reached this less manageable size do we see the fruitful, healing, and revivifying effects it has on the wilderness and eventually the Dead Sea.

As a young Christian and later as a young pastor, I felt as if I had my life and my ministry pretty well figured out. God was kind enough to use my efforts for his good purposes, but those were not years of great or lasting fruit. As my life journey has continued, I have had so many more moments when I felt far beyond my depth. At those moments, my sense of dependence far exceeded any illusion of being in control of things. In fact, through the years, it's been when I move beyond my depth that God's Spirit does more in me and often in the situation than I ever imagined. In these cases hu-mility is no longer just an appropriate posture to take; it is the only posture that makes any sense.

Finally, I'm struck by the simplicity of the question the man asks Ezekiel in verse 6: "Do you see this?" This is not a question about whether Ezekiel remembered to wear his glasses. Instead, it's a question of perception. God was inviting Ezekiel to do more than take a hurried glance at what was before him. God invited Ezekiel to gaze into the spiritual reality being revealed, to see with his heart what he's seeing with his eyes. We all are invited. It strikes me that Ezekiel should have been easily able to look back up river and see the temple, the source of this river. Surely that would have had profound implications for his understanding of what was happening right in front of him. He was witnessing the flow of living water that had its beginning in the Presence. Yet too often I also fail to see with my heart because of hurry, anxiety, or even shame.

A PLACE OF RENEWAL

After seeing the temple and the river that flows from it, we come to a scene of renewal (Ezek 47:7-12). A long line of fruit trees grows on either side of this refreshing river. What was once a dead sea is quite literally resurrected. What was unproductive becomes fruitful beyond measure. Vitality abounds. Healing and renewal come. What if this river were to flow through you, bringing life in place of death, refreshment in place of thirst and drought, healing in place of brokenness and disorder, fruitfulness in place of barrenness? What a vision!

> When I arrived there, I saw a great number of trees on each side of the river. He said to me, "This water flows toward the eastern region and goes down into the Arabah, where it enters the Dead Sea. When it empties into the sea, the salty water there becomes fresh. Swarms of living creatures will live wherever the river flows. There will be large numbers of fish, because this water flows there and makes the salt water fresh; so where the river flows everything will live. Fishermen will stand along the shore; from En Gedi to

En Eglaim there will be places for spreading nets. The fish will be of many kinds—like the fish of the Mediterranean Sea. But the swamps and marshes will not become fresh; they will be left for salt. Fruit trees of all kinds will grow on both banks of the river. Their leaves will not wither, nor will their fruit fail. Every month they will bear fruit, because the water from the sanctuary flows to them. Their fruit will serve for food and their leaves for healing." (Ezek 47:7-12)

Everything that happens downriver from where the man stood with Ezekiel is future focused. Where the river eventually empties into the Dead Sea, the salty water becomes fresh. Swarms of living creatures will come alive wherever the river flows. Fish will abound then, and fishermen will again make a living. Fruit trees will grow where there had been barren desert. This is a holy vision of future good that the flowing river will bring. Ezekiel didn't see everything the man said about this future, but he heard it and trusted what he heard. It's likely that a person would not be able to see the temple from the point at which trees grow along the river, and certainly not from the spot where it entered the Dead Sea. But what may be absent in vision is present in effect. The temple may not be visible, but its impact is seen everywhere here.

This vision echoes David's language in Psalm 1:3 about trees whose leaves do not wither and whose fruit never fails. This river of living water gives certainty to the vitality and fruitfulness Ezekiel witnessed. Instead of a single, annual yield of fruit, this river enables a continual fruitfulness. Also, after the land is healed (v. 8), it provides trees with leaves that bring healing. Jesus' parallel statement that "rivers of living water flow from within" in John 7:38 offers two further insights.

First, rivers of living water flow from those who believe in Jesus. This flow of life begins with the simple response of trust. When my own anxiety or impulse to prove myself is fueling me, the gate through which living water would flow is obstructed. Too often my response is to just try harder. But what if I learned to reopen that gate of trust and redirect my attention and devotion to the one who calls himself "living water"? I hear in my head a voice complaining, *But that's too simple. The world is more complex than that.* And while I have to agree, I also have to ask whether my best strategy is in fact to engage in all that complexity from the place of my own self-reliance or, worse, self-importance. Rather than lean on my own interpretation of what's happening around me and my own strategy for dealing with it, perhaps I could instead find a way to trust in the Lord more fully in a way that would allow divine life to fill me and flow through me to bless others.

Second, the thirst that draws a person to Jesus becomes a *river* of living water. What was emptiness becomes fullness to the point of overflow. Furthermore, the reason we can open up to Jesus about our real thirst is that he will not only satisfy it but transform us into those through whom living water might flow to help quench the thirsts of others. As the river of God's presence flows through our worshiping and abiding lives, we experience healing that can become a source of healing for others. Ministry is sharing the fruit of God's transforming work in our own lives. My most fruitful ministry occurs when I am able to share the growing reality of God's presence within me for the benefit of another.

In Ezekiel's vision a river empties into the Dead Sea and transforms it. One of the saltiest of water bodies on earth becomes fresh and life sustaining. (The average salt content of ocean water is about 3.5 percent. The salt content at the Dead Sea has recently been measured at about 34 percent.) Not even the mightiest of rivers on earth manage to affect, much less transform, the oceans into which they flow. Instead, every single river ends up being changed from fresh to salty. Only a river sourced in God's presence could change the sea. Similarly, no one's life is so bitter, sour, or salty that God's Spirit cannot flow into it and make it fresh.

ENCOUNTERING THE DEAD SEA

When we encounter places in our lives or our work that are more dead sea than living water, we can too easily forget the temple and the river. When that happens, we try to manage those wilderness or dead sea places ourselves. We forget to go to the temple and abide in the realities of God with us and of God's Spirit flowing within us. Our abiding brings the life of God's kingdom to where we live and engage our leadership roles. This helps us lead from great abundance and in deeper trust.

Instead of looking up to God at the start, we focus our attention on the wounded places that need healing, the dry places that need refreshment, the dead places that need new life, the barren places that need to be made fruitful once more. However, in the language of the vision, all of the healing outcomes are described in the future tense, beyond the seer's vision. Only the temple and the river are in the present tense. Sometimes our busyness causes us to lose sight of the temple. Sometimes we get so excited about the work we're doing for God that we forget the God we are serving.

The instinct of many leaders is to focus first on solving the problems of dryness and deadness that we see. How do we cause more inspiration, refreshment, energy, direction, and strategic vision to come to the dry and dead places? Then, when we have an idea, we work on squeezing more out of what is before us, often with strategies like more rules, accountability, and exhortation. But those around us usually feel more drained than energized.

Based on our limited perspective, we set about finding a solution to the problem of the dead sea we discern. We seek to manage the problem locally. Drawing on our experience, training, and immediate resources, we work frantically to solve the problem before us. These efforts are usually the expression of a good heart and genuine concern. The problem lies not in our intention but in our approach. When we feel overwhelmed by the wilderness before us, we might be tempted to pretend the situation is not as bad as it seems. Or we decorate the desert so it looks nice even if it's still dry and mostly dead. But the best option steers our attention first to the temple and then to the living water that flows from it. Our looking to God, our awareness of his presence and the availability of his power, brings to the wilderness and to the dead sea something new.

How does this speak to our experience today, especially when it comes to the church? Douglas Steere, a Quaker professor and author, wrote these words fifty years ago about the busyness he witnessed among Christians when they gathered:

> In religious circles we find today a fierce and almost violent planning and programming, a sense that without ceaseless activity nothing will ever be accomplished. How seldom it occurs to us that God has to undo and to do all over again so much of what we in our willfulness have pushed through in his name. How little there is in us of the silent and radiant strength in which the secret works of God really take place! How ready we are to speak, how loathe to listen, to sense the further dimension of what it is that we confront.

These words are just as true today. Instead of living and serving in the presence of a God who is always at work and from whom flows abundance, we work almost violently, as though no work but our own would make a difference. We forget that God is already working and that we would be wise to simply join him in that work. And whatever work God is doing, he does so in a way that is in keeping with who he is: gentle, kind, patient, peaceful. When we are working *with* God, we also will work with gentleness, kindness, patience, and peace.

LIVING IN THE OVERFLOW

When it comes to working with God in leadership, spiritual formation and leadership development are too often inversely related. This is not as it *should* be, but it's a pattern I've noticed much too often—sometimes, unfortunately, in my own experience. Leaders are either wilderness-focused with little temple awareness, or they are temple-parked with little wilderness engagement.

In the Sermon on the Mount Jesus invites us to seek first God's kingdom and God's righteousness (Mt 6:33), knowing that we will find everything we truly need for our lives and our work. When we see brokenness in our lives or in the lives of those we care about, are we to seek restoration and renewal? Of course, but not first. When we see dryness, are we to seek refreshment? Of course, but not first. We are to first seek God—his good reign in our lives and our leadership roles. This seeking is the means by which a river of living water begins to flow.

When I see a situation that needs what the life of God might bring to it, how do I respond? No one has to squeeze water out of leaders who truly seek God first. They come with their own internal water source. Something within them is so alive and holy that they can't contain it. Living water flows out to bless and benefit people around them. That's leadership from divine overflow rather than leadership from managed meagerness. And I envision divine overflow as key to unhurried leadership.

What does this overflow look like? Unhurried leaders create environments within which people flourish. Pastors create environments in which members of the community are able to deepen their roots in Jesus, and pastors then share that life in community with those they serve. Supervisors provide space for their team members to try new things. Unhurried leaders provide people an opportunity to learn to move in the flow of God's life, God's love, and God's guidance.

In his book *The Spiritual Formation of Leaders,* my friend and mentor Chuck Miller used the simple metaphor of Soul Room and Leadership Room to talk about the holy rhythms of spiritual formation and leadership. Visualize the Soul Room as the central room where personal engagement and encounter with God takes place. The Leadership Room surrounds the Soul Room and contains all of our relationships, tasks, projects, and activities. Blending this metaphor with the Ezekiel 47 vision (Soul Room = temple; Leadership Room = wilderness or dead sea) will reveal a few ways these rooms might relate.

One option is the "seek leadership first" approach. This is where leaders set up shop in the wilderness and frantically try to directly solve the problems they find. There is little sense, if any, of a temple or a river of living water flowing from the temple to where the leaders work.

Second is the "seek formation first" approach. Here, a leader is so blessed to have found the temple that he doesn't want to leave. Certain meaningful spiritual practices or a supportive formational community have become so personally life giving that the temple becomes the leader's whole world. Again, there is little sense—if any—of a river or a wilderness or a dead sea where leaders might share what they are being given in the temple.

Third comes the "Soul Room, then Leadership Room" approach. Here, a leader enjoys a rich engagement with God in the temple, gets in his car, drives down to the wilderness or the dead sea, and goes to work—with little memory of his time in the temple and little connection to the reality of God within him. Again, there is little sense of a river connecting the temple to the wilderness or dead sea. Too often in our experience, the Soul Room and the Leadership Room are separate and unrelated.

One more option remains, and you won't be surprised that I call this approach "overflow leadership." Here, leaders have an integrated awareness of God's beautiful and abundant presence *and* the great need that surrounds them. The organic connection between these two realities is the river. God would like to bless us with abundance, healing, restoration, and refreshment that will then flow through us to bless and benefit those around us. This is the vital engagement that unhurried leaders can provide to the world around them and what I will talk about in the rest of this book.

Now, when I talk about overflow leadership, I'm not necessarily talking about *feeling* full but about learning to live in *trusted* fullness. For example, I do not always feel full of inspiration or courage when I stand to speak before an unfamiliar group. I often come to those moments feeling full of nerves or tongue-tied. I've learned to trust that fullness is present even when I don't feel it. I stand to speak believing that the good this group needs will be available to and through me as I stand and not necessarily anytime sooner. This way has cultivated a deeper trust in God as it relates to how I do ministry in other ways.

I love how Thomas Kelly, a Quaker spiritual author, envisions this sort of overflow of life from God into a needy world, echoing the imagery of Ezekiel 47:

> Now out from such a holy Center come the commissions of life. Our fellowship with God issues in world concern. We cannot keep the love of God to ourselves. It spills over. It quickens us. It makes us see the world's need anew. We love people, and we grieve to see them blind when they might be seeing, asleep with all the world's comforts when they ought to be awake and living sacrificially, accepting the world's goods as their right when they really hold them only in temporary trust. It is because from this holy Center we relove people, relove our neighbors as ourselves, that we are bestirred to be means of their awakening. The deepest human need is not food and clothing and shelter, important as they are. It is God.

Yes, the deepest human need truly is God.

PRACTICE: *PRAYER OF INTENTION*

You might want to try praying this prayer, or writing an overflow prayer of your own.

Jesus, I desire that the holy passion in my heart and at my core, where you've made yourself at home, would find a point of outward flow. I long for those rivers of your Spirit's living water—sourced in those places of trustful abiding—to pour out of me. Open a way for such a flow. I do acknowledge ways in which I have willfully blocked that flow. Reveal to me ways I have unwillingly blocked that flow. And change me so I no longer block the flow intentionally and unintentionally. I ask, Lord, that from this day forward my life and leadership will be fruitful. Apart from you, that cannot happen, but I am blessed to not be apart from you. The temple of your presence within me is real; the river of your life flowing from me is real. Thank you—and use me for the good of your people and your great glory. Amen.

Unhurried Leadership Reflections

1. In what aspects of your life do you feel dry? What relationships are less lush than you wish? In what specific ways is your ministry or work not as fruitful as you had envisioned? What solutions have you tried? How well have they worked?

2. Which of the Soul Room/Leadership Room configurations above reflects your own experience? In what ways is God inviting, nudging, or compelling you to integrate these rooms in your life?

3. At this place in your life, what can you do to better seek God first? What thirsts do you find within yourself that might be a clue as to how you might come to him?

4. Do you identify with having a strong sense of temple—of God's presence—in your life but not an equally strong sense of how the reality of God-with-you flows into the work of your life? Talk to God about this sense of dis-integration. Ask God about how you might move forward with greater integration.

5. What are some of the dead sea places where you long to see fresh life, lasting fruit, and true healing in your own life? In your family or among your friends? In your workplace or ministry places? What will you do in addition to praying?

THREE

Leading in His Presence

WHEN I WAS A YOUNG PASTOR, I had a passion to help people walk closely with God. I wanted them to grow deep roots. The problem was that I really didn't know how to do this. I was being mentored in how to study and teach compellingly from the Scriptures. I was being coached in many practical planning competencies of ministry. But I wasn't being led in how to walk with God as a pastor and then to shepherd others in such a journey. My walk with God was largely assumed and focused attention was given to developing teaching or ministry managing skills.

I was reading many books on spiritual growth and prayer and then passing that information along in my teaching. But it didn't seem to make much difference in the lives of those I was shepherding. The true ideas I was transferring from books to teaching hadn't found a home in me yet. It took a number of years before God graciously brought a few men into my life who were practiced in a way of leadership that was deep-rooted and fruitful in helping others deepen their roots. They showed me how to actually walk with God as a pastor. They showed me by example how to love and serve people in ways that actually attracted them to walking with God in their own lives. They became friends, brothers, mentors, even fathers to me. I witnessed leaders who were gifted and humble, zealous and gentle, fruitful and unselfish. I witnessed their lives and learned from them. They lived what I had, up until then, only read about.

What I learned about leadership in all this is that we are led before we lead.

Isaiah 55:1-3 has given some shape to this insight for me. I've been learning how to lead others even as I myself am led by God's presence, aware of and dependent on the initiative and engagement of God with me.

> Come, all you who are thirsty,
>   come to the waters;
> and you who have no money,
>   come, buy and eat!
> Come, buy wine and milk
>   without money and without cost.
> Why spend money on what is not bread,
>   and your labor on what does not satisfy?
> Listen, listen to me, and eat what is good,
>   and you will delight in the richest of fare.
> Give ear and come to me;
>   listen, that you may live.
> I will make an everlasting covenant with you,
>   my faithful love promised to David.

In this brief passage, I hear four key words of invitation: *come, listen, buy,* and *eat.* Notice the sequence and the flow of these words: they encourage us to come to God, listen to him, trust him, and enjoy him. *Come* is an invitation to presence and communion; *listen,* an invitation to conversation and learning; *buy,* to trusting and entrusting; and *eat,* to contemplation and nourishment.

COME

God first extends a very simple invitation. It's the word most invitations to a special event or a party use to draw us in: *come*. You are invited. You are wanted. You are welcome. God wants us to come close to him; he invites us to draw near. Few things feel as good as being wanted by someone significant. When a person I admire invites me to join her for a meal or a special gathering, I feel appreciated and honored, recognized and special.

This Isaiah 55 invitation has been extended to you and me by the eternal one, the King of kings, the Almighty. God wants to include us in what he is doing in history, what he is doing in the world today. God wants us close to him, entering into and enjoying his presence. Coming to God like this implies that, like Peter, Andrew, James, and John, who left their fishing boats behind to follow Jesus, we are willing to leave behind whatever is necessary to more closely follow Jesus. These four disciples responded to the fundamental invitation of the gospel: *Come to me. Come, follow me.*

Now, notice some specifics about the people God invites to come to him. The pure and holy God extends his invitation to "all you who are thirsty" and to "you who have no money." God invites us to come when we are thirsty—and whether or not we feel we can afford whatever he has that might quench our thirst. So, for what am I thirsty? How about you? We're not talking about mere physical dehydration, as serious as that problem can be. We are talking about the deepest desires of our heart.

God appeals to those deepest and truest desires of our hearts. So what thirsts have been the target of God's invitation to me? Sometimes I've been anxious and thirsty for peace; despairing and thirsty for hope; discouraged and thirsty for encouragement; lonely and thirsty for companionship; or hurting and thirsty for comfort. The key question is this: *Where am I taking my thirsts?* I've too often made the mistake of denying that I'm thirsty. (When I do that, my thirsts—in quest of satisfaction—sneak out at unexpected and even inappropriate times or places, so I don't advise that approach.) Or I've taken my thirsts to places or things that will never satisfy, although they do seem to help in the moment . . . for a moment.

I have, for example, sometimes taken my thirst for peace to places of escape. Rather than coming to the Prince of Peace and resting in his presence, I've tried to hide from unpleasant anxiety through self-distraction or some other form of numbing behavior. It didn't work. I gave in to the temptation to run away from my thirst for deep peace and instead hide myself in more and more activity. Or when I've thirsted for security, I have found myself tempted to try quenching that thirst by acquiring more possessions, adding more achievements to my résumé, or fostering in others more good opinions of me. These things help a little, but only in the moment. They don't quench my thirst for long.

Now notice that whatever our thirst may be, we are invited to come *to the waters*. God invites us to come to him thirsty. He has water for us that will quench whatever thirst we bring. To be more specific, God offers himself as the source of refreshment for any thirsty ones who come. And Jesus promised that because we believe in him, this living water that is sourced in him will flow forth from within us to bless others (Jn 7:38).

This image of living water flowing reminds me of visiting Israel with my wife a few years ago. Day after day, our tour guide pointed out something about an aqueduct, a *mikveh* (a Jewish bath used for ritual cleansing), or a cistern. People in Israel have always had to pay good attention to capturing and preserving water. Their creativity and resourcefulness extend back centuries because of how dry the land of Israel is. And it was in this dry land that God spoke to his people of bringing him our thirsts and finding in him all the refreshment we could desire.

And—even better—this refreshment won't cost us. Don't you love being invited somewhere and being told to come without money? God isn't inviting me out to dinner and then expecting me to pay the bill. God is inviting me to a party in his home—and of course God is picking up the tab. This is God's language of grace. So, when I accept his invitation, I am coming into the presence of a generous God to receive blessings from him rather than coming into the presence of a demanding God who requires me to pay a debt that is beyond what I can possibly afford.

Jesus invites us to come to him and follow him, but sometimes I am more focused only on where I am *going*. We travel here, have an appointment there, and attend a meeting after that. Going here and going there. We are always going! And of course leaders go. Leaders take initiative. Leaders act. And quite understandably our first thought as leaders is often what we are going to *do*. This action orientation is a valuable gift. But we are not to lead alone, in our own power, according to our best thoughts, so we cannot fixate on this gift of doing; we need to also open those gifts that bring us into deeper communion with the one who is the great leader, the one who longs to lead with us. We will lead better when we lead in the presence of our King.

Yes, our leadership is too often mostly in terms of *go*: Go to meetings. Go to serve. Go, go, go! But the first invitation to us leaders is always Jesus' *come*. We learn to go with Jesus only after we come to him and grow in following him. Long before I go to the ends of the earth for the gospel, Jesus invites me to come to him. And that brings us to the next invitation: when I accept his invitation to come, he then invites me to listen.

LISTEN

As I write these words, I've been given the gift of a place to stay in the mountains above Jarabacoa in the Dominican Republic where I just finished leading a retreat for leaders. Before I leave for home, I'm staying a few more days to write. As I take a moment to listen, I immediately notice the wind moving through the surrounding trees. I hear the melody of the chimes as that same wind cools the patio. I hear the sound of some men digging holes for new posts for a barbed wire fence that has grown old and rotted with time. From every direction I hear a number of birds singing. Take a moment to listen to the sounds around you right now. What do you hear? A computer fan or some other electric whir? A conversation? Are vehicles going here and there nearby? What do you hear?

Now let's consider a deeper kind of listening. What do we hear when we pay attention to our hearts and minds? I hear concern about whether or not I'll get a first draft written by my due date (I didn't). I hear excitement about seeing my family tomorrow after a long absence. I hear gratitude for the gift of this place and this time. Listen to your own thoughts right now. Are those thoughts anxious or peaceful, angry or gentle, fearful or confident, self-condemning or self-accepting?

Having come to Jesus, we are invited to listen not just to nature sounds, neighborhood sounds, office sounds, or even the sound of our own thoughts, but to a person: Jesus says, "Listen to *me*." He invites us to a place where we rest our mouths before God and open our ears. That's not easy to do in our busy, noisy world, but it's sure good.

Jesus invites us to come to the Scriptures, for instance, and to listen. Sometimes we have our own agendas—questions to be answered, problems to be solved, cases to be proven—when we open the Bible. But God invites us to engage the Scriptures in a relational and conversational way. God's Word is a living word because when we read it, we engage with its living author. We are not just reading nice words from a time long ago and a land far away.

I think of the description of the Berean Jews. Luke said they were of more noble character than the ones in Thessolonica for one very simple reason: "They received the message with great eagerness and examined the Scriptures every day to see if what Paul said was true" (Acts 17:11).

The Bereans listened. But—perhaps not surprisingly—in my own conservative evangelical past, this verse from Acts 17 was used to support passionate and daily Bible study. That encouragement is valid as far as it goes, but the study of Scripture needs to be a listening and receptive sort of study. I am to study God's Word in order to be taught by him. I am to choose to be receptive to what God wants me to understand.

The Jews of Thessalonica, however, were not listeners. The historical context indicates that they were fine with rounding up unsavory characters to riot and use violence to protest what Paul was saying. After all, they saw him as a threat to their position, one that they were unwilling to examine in light of the Scriptures. The Thessalonians' assumptions and expectations crowded out the simple truth of what Paul was declaring, explaining, and even proving. That proof of the validity of the apostle's message meant nothing to them. They were bent on defending their pre-existing beliefs that carried the weight of (misguided) tradition. Defensive and protective of their vision of God, the Thessalonians were fine with completely disregarding the counsel of God. They were not listeners.

But the Bereans were. At whatever personal cost, the Berean Jews were willing to listen and seek God for a vision of his character and his way even though what they learned might contradict much that they had believed before. Doing so is not easy for any of us. Oh, it's easy to listen when what we hear corresponds to what we already think. But I think we are tempted to be more Thessalonian than Berean. We've believed certain things about God and his ways for years, maybe decades, and then someone comes along suggesting that our vision of God has been misguided on certain points. Are we so invested in our past experience that we aren't willing to be a listener in the present?

Underscoring the importance of listening, God says that if we listen, we will live (Isaiah 55:3). I can't help but think of Jesus' words in the wilderness. Having fasted for forty days, he is tempted by the devil to make miracle bread for himself from the stones. Jesus replies to this suggestion with a line from the law: "It is written: 'Man shall not live on bread alone, but on every word that comes from the mouth of God'" (Mt 4:4). If we listen well as we engage in conversation with the Father, we will hear words of life. So as we come to God, we are wise to be attentive, receptive, listening, and responsive.

And I'm preaching to myself here. As a leader, I do a lot of talking on the job—I talk on the phone, during appointments, in counseling sessions, on retreats, and at conferences. The temptation I face is to turn everything in the Christian life and in my work into what I say, or they say, or someone says. But the first act Jesus invites us to do once we come is to listen. This pattern applies to prayer as well as Bible study. For far too long I assumed that prayer was only the words I say to God. Remember our breathing exercise? We try exhaling, then exhaling again and again. It doesn't work, but I keep finding myself trying to make it work. Prayer invites us to inhale, to listen.

So, having come to God and listened, we are then invited to "buy." What does that look like?

BUY

In everyday conversation, we can use the word *buy* to mean believe: "I buy that" or "I don't buy that at all." In that context, we're not talking about spending money; we're talking about trust. We either do or do not believe that what another person has said is true. We either put confidence in what we've heard, or we don't. Similarly, in the process outlined in Isaiah 55, we come to God, and then we listen. Having heard whatever God communicated to us through Scripture, by his Spirit, through a friend or using whatever other means he wishes, we then face this very simple and practical decision: "Do I *buy* it?"

Buy is the language of personal investment, commitment, or trust. Now, I have heard many good things over the years I've been a follower of Jesus. These days my great need is to remember what I know . . . and buy it again! Isaiah's invitation applies to me: he invites me to buy wine and milk—without money! We can buy what we most need—peace, courage, refreshment, nourishment, whatever—not with money but with ourselves. God invites us into places of deeper personal engagement, investment, and dependence on him.

This is one of the places where I most easily get stuck. I listen to and perhaps agree, in theory, with something good I hear in Scripture or in a sermon, but I don't let myself believe and trust what I've heard. I get stuck between the listening and the buying. I fail to trust what I claim to believe. And I'm not addressing semantics here; I'm addressing my resistance.

Arguing voices rise up encouraging me to disagree with what I hear from God. Whispers of "Yes but" emerge from the back of my mind and the shadows of my heart. When, for example, I hear Jesus say, very simply, that my life does *not* consist in the abundance of my possessions (Lk 12:15), my objections are immediate. "But life really *would* be better, wouldn't it, with a new computer to replace that old, heavy, slow thing I'm typing on now. And what if I owned a house closer to the ocean? That would definitely improve my life!" So which voice do I choose to heed? Which voice do I trust? Which do I *buy*? Either my deepest, truest life is found in communion with the one who calls himself Life, or the richest life possible is "out there" somewhere else and I need to hurry up to pursue, find, and acquire it.

Another example of my resistant nature comes when I read Philippians 4:6-7. There Paul wrote that I don't need to be anxious about anything because I can pray about everything, and that such ongoing prayer would secure my heart against the worries that so often overtake me. But another whispering voice argues with that truth from God's Word: "Yes, but how will anyone know whether you truly care if you don't worry a lot?" I hear the wise, good, beautiful voice of God, but do I trust what I hear and entrust myself to his life-giving guidance? I'll talk more about this matter of noticing our thoughts in a later chapter.

Before we leave this discussion of buying, I find it interesting that our passage in Isaiah contains only one question: "Why spend money on what is not bread, and your labor on what does not satisfy?" Why indeed! Why do I buy what is *not* bread? Why do I spend myself on what does not nourish or even satisfy me? I am allowing my operative and therefore actual beliefs to be at odds with what I claim to believe about God, his kingdom, and his ways. So I should not be surprised that this kind of existence neither fills nor satisfies me. I could choose to spend myself on what would both truly satisfy me *and* enable me to bless others. I could if, by God's grace, I would.

But too often in my roles as a Christian leader, I run past God's invitation to buy, to trust him, and instead I become a salesman. I try to sell people on the value of a meeting that I've planned and want them to attend. Sell, sell, sell. When my influence is not rooted in my own deep trust in the good things God has said, my selling becomes manipulative and self-serving. I find myself wanting to sell people on my perspective rather than inviting them to trust the One I myself am coming to trust more deeply. I might find myself guilty of—in the words of Eugene Peterson— "[conspiring] to get [people] involved in anything and everything they think will be good for their souls and good for the church. Well-intentioned but dead wrong. All the leaders do is get them so busy for the Lord that they have no time for the Lord, pour in so much information about God that they never have a chance to listen to God." As a leader, I'm tempted to get people to buy something from *me* rather than from God.

If I'm honest with myself, I seem to have a more positive kingdom influence on people as I more deeply trust what God has said to me, as I surrender more completely to God in loving dependence on him. Henri Nouwen said that "what is most personal is also most universal." When we come to deep places of personal trust in Christ, we will be most able to encourage and guide others in their own deepening trust.

So having come to God as a listener and arrived at places of deeper trust, what comes next?

EAT AND DELIGHT

Consider the four words of invitation in terms of a grocery store. We won't get much nourishment if we don't first *come* in through the doors of the local market, put good food into our carts (*listen*), and then *buy* what we gathered. But all that activity won't help us if we don't *eat* and *enjoy* the good food we take home.

Eat is the invitation to take in and be nourished by the good things we receive in our conversational relationship with God. I've included the word *delight* since I think it goes well with *eat*. We're not talking about bare sustenance here, but about a holy feast. The psalmist said it well: "I will be fully satisfied as with the richest of foods" (Ps 63:5). Instead of filling ourselves with what Isaiah said is "not bread," we "delight in the richest of fare." We can eat as well as delight in the good and nourishing words we hear when we spend time with God, or we can eat things of this world that actually make us hungrier. Which do we choose? We are invited to digest the good words God gives us, to soak in them, meditate on them, integrate them into our thinking, incorporate them in our lives, and enjoy them as the blessing they are.

Nourishment can sound so simple, but I interact with a lot of malnourished leaders. I'm not talking about leaders in under-developed countries who do not have enough food on their tables. I'm talking about leaders in economically wealthy parts of the world who forget to feed their own souls. They just get too busy. As a result, they are starving when they take on their leadership roles and responsibilities. They seek nourishment in whatever they might accomplish for God. Such leaders expect—perhaps unknowingly—the people they serve to give them something that will satisfy their soul. They enter into leadership with an empty cup, wanting something out there to fill it, when they have another and better option. These leaders could come, listen, buy, and drink what is good. The

Lord would fill their cup to overflowing. Then their leadership would be an expression of soul abundance rather than an exercise in deficit spending.

What I find strange about myself are those times when I've had a pantry full of great food—good readings, good teachings, and good insights—that I simply didn't eat and enjoy. It's as though I collected all this good nourishment only to give it to others; I never took it in for myself as well. But I don't want to be like the chef who doesn't enjoy his own cooking anymore. I want to take delight in the goodness and tastiness of what I am sharing with others. I find such delight when my deepest hungers meet God's abundant provision. Also, I know I lead more effectively when I lead out of plenty rather than out of want.

When I am delighting in my Father's good and nourishing words, I find myself blessed with contentment and satisfaction. Have you noticed that it's very hard to tempt a satisfied person? When we are well nourished by all the good things God provides, when we are as satisfied in our soul as we might be having just eaten and enjoyed our very favorite meal, temptation does not have nearly the same power over us. But when we are starving our souls—even if our starvation is the result of some misguided sense of devotion, commitment, or sacrifice—false food entices.

Obedience to Paul's simple invitation and instruction to "rejoice always" (1 Thess 5:16) enables us to resist the temptation to false food. In my experience, it has helped to hear this as an invitation to "rejoice *now*." I can choose joy now, even in the midst of feelings of anxiety, frustration, loss, or whatever. And that choice of joy can contribute to my sense of contentment and satisfaction.

So, as for eating and delighting, make sure you're eating. As a leader, especially in my pastoral roles through the years, I have sometimes found myself first feeding others but not feeding myself. And I think of that unhealthy tendency every time I'm on a plane and the flight attendant does the "put your own oxygen mask on first" routine. Those words are wise and spot-on counsel for those of us who are in positions of spiritual leadership—and we ignore that wisdom at our own peril.

JESUS AND HIS FRIENDS

One morning, when I was coming to God, I found myself drawn to Mark 8:11-26. There, Jesus warned the disciples about the yeast of the Pharisees (a warning about the godlessness of the religious person) and the yeast of Herod (a warning about the godlessness of the worldly person). The disciples, however, thought Jesus was talking about their failure to bring bread to eat on the journey. Jesus responded by asking the Twelve whether their eyes could see and their ears, hear. When Jesus asked them, "Do you not yet understand?" he was essentially asking them, "Are you listening?"

If I had been one of those disciples, I'm pretty sure I would have missed Jesus' meaning as well. I might have realized he was saying something about the difference between bodily food and soul food. But I might have been talking about lunch when Jesus was talking about kingdom provision. Jesus reminded the disciples that at least twice God had blessed their little bit of bread so that it fed thousands. The point is as relevant today as it was then: the power of God's kingdom is present to provide good and needed things. Abundance is available for kingdom service. And when I live my life listening and trusting that God's very real kingdom is near, I experience provision that can only be explained as evidence of his infinite grace.

I see in Jesus' words about the Pharisees and Herod, though, the reality that there are both nonreligious and religious ways to live distant from God, to fail to come and listen, trust and enjoy him. So I find myself praying, "Jesus, I am so much like your first disciples. I become so focused on what I need for my physical life (whether I'll have enough money often rises to the top of that list) that I fail to live in the real abundance of your kingdom. You are inviting me to make coming to you and listening to you my first response rather than my last resort. After all, if you can take a little boy's few loaves and multiply them to feed a town-sized crowd, why wouldn't I surrender to you my little talents, my little treasures, my brief lifetime, and let you multiply them in a way that provides far more good than one life, by itself, could ever do?"

When I don't first go to Jesus with, for instance, my thirst for recognition, I end up taking that thirst to the crowd. Coming to the crowd for what I need is a gamble at best.

Although I am encouraged by moments of affirmation when I speak somewhere or by words of appreciation for something I've written, that recognition pales compared to the loving attention and joyous affirmation of Father and Son by the Spirit. That is *real* bread and *real* drink.

To counter this temptation I pray: "Teach me, Jesus. Speak bracing words to me that will awaken me from my soul sleepiness. Show me how to abide in the realities of your kingdom in a way that allows my life to reflect your abundance and to overflow with your goodness and grace." Such would be kingdom leadership—leadership out of abundance rather than scarcity.

PRACTICE: *LISTENING IN THE MORNING*

So what does this come-listen-buy-eat rhythm look like on a typical morning? I love rising early before my wife or sons. The morning is quiet. I make myself a delicious cup of home-roasted coffee. I sit in our library or on the back patio, unhurriedly sipping. Sometimes I'll just listen to the sounds of creation—birds singing, a breeze blowing. Rather than a luxury I can hardly afford because of my many responsibilities, this window of time is an important "temple" moment for me as I begin my day.

Often in my morning time with God I will read from the Scriptures and, if something captures my attention, journal a thought or a prayer in response. I try to do this leisurely; I want to savor the goodness of these moments in the Lord's presence. After the reading, I'll often take fifteen minutes sitting quietly to reflect on and abide with something God gave me from the Scriptures. It may be simply a word, a short phrase, or a single line, but I seek to live with it and let it soak into my thoughts and affect my emotions. I'm not trying to dissect the words from Scripture or examine them from a distance. I'm simply seeking to abide with the good word God has given me. My hope is that this truth will stay with me through the day, coming to the forefront of my mind in a moment of need, coming forth to nourish me, guide me, or encourage me. And, yes, some mornings present more of a challenge to this routine than others, but my intention is to come, listen, buy, and eat before I start each day.

So Jesus has sent the invitation. He invites us to come and listen. He invites us to trust that there are good things to eat and enjoy in God's presence. And when we are blessed with those good things, we can be a blessing to others.

Leading in God's presence means learning to slow down to a pace that doesn't weaken our rootedness in the richness of all God is, a pace that enables us to bear the fruit of God's presence in all we are becoming and all we are doing. We are to live at a slow enough pace that we are able to taste eternity and share it with others.

Unhurried Leadership Reflections

1. Look again at the words of invitation: *come, listen, buy, eat.* Which word seems to most capture the invitation you sense at this place in your journey with God? Which word seems to most touch your current hungers and thirsts? Take a few moments to respond to this invitation in prayer.

2. What are you thirsty for right now? Or, put differently, where do you feel dissatisfied, unfulfilled, anxious, or fearful? How might

you take this thirst to God right now? How might you let him know in very honest language just how thirsty you feel? What might God want to do to quench your thirst? Ask. And what might God want you to do to quench your thirst in a spiritually healthy way? Again, ask.

3. Where do you see yourself spending money—or time or effort—in ways that have led not to nourishment or satisfaction but rather to greater hunger and thirst? Talk to God about this. Ask him to enable you to come to him and then truly listen to him.

4. How long has it been since you recognized God's invitation into his presence? If it has been awhile, take a moment now to reread Isaiah 55:1-3, personalizing the verses by inserting your name there. As you read this passage, hear the words as God's personal invitation to you rather than as a general invitation for everyone.

5. Some leaders want to go somewhere *for* God rather than coming *to* God first. When, if ever, are you tempted to run past God in order to serve him? Those are moments when God would welcome you to come first and listen.

FOUR

Vision of God, Vision from God

YEARS AGO, WHEN OUR CHILDREN were in grade school, I stepped away from all my paid ministry and work positions to take a one-year sabbatical. As that year began, we embarked on a six-week, three-thousand-mile road trip from our home in California through seven Western states to visit family and friends, to enjoy beautiful scenery, and to let my soul breathe. Our sons were small enough to fit on a single bench seat of our Ford Aerostar van. It's a fond memory especially in light of the fact that our sons can now grow impressive facial hair.

I was the primary driver on that trip. When my wife, Gem, or our sons went into nap mode, I would watch the scenery. I tried to resist the inner temptation to race to the destination and sought instead to relax into an "enjoy the journey" mode and mindset. When I managed to slow down inside, these long drives became restful, playful, and restorative opportunities.

In my mind's eye, I can still see the long, straight drive of Interstate 5 through the San Joaquin Valley in Central California. Along those seemingly unending stretches of highway, I see grassy fields, to both my left and right, whizzing by in a blur. I don't see much detail or gain much perspective looking at what is near me when I'm traveling at 65 mph. As I look a bit ahead instead of glancing out the side window, I do see upcoming exits and nearby natural features. From my perspective, though, they are moving, just not with as much blur or hurry. But in the midst of the visual rush happening immediately around me, if I look a bit farther ahead, I see on the horizon quiet, restful clouds and mountains fixed in the distance. I discover a simple and solitary stillness if I raise my gaze only a few degrees.

In the midst of my many and varied activities, a vision of God becomes that steady and stable horizon. Living my life and doing my work means full and busy days. Thankfully, my vision *of* God offers a stable background for my vision *from* God in the foreground—a vision for some good work I want to do to honor God's kingdom.

Not many years after this sabbatical journey, our family was able to visit Oahu. At the time my brother flew for Aloha Airlines, and my father owned a condominium in Waikiki. On our tight ministry budget, we were grateful for the opportunity to spend family time in Hawaii. One day our family went to visit Hanauma Bay, which many believe to be the most beautiful snorkeling location in Hawaii. What I remember was fighting the waves when I was trying to swim at the surface. In this wrestling match, I sometimes felt like I was breathing in more saltwater than air! But when I dived down below the waves and let my flippers take me down to deeper places, I found quiet. The surface was turbulent; the deep was calm. Similarly, those of us who follow Jesus have a depth beneath us, under every crashing wave of busyness, that can be a secure place for our anxious souls.

And what do road trips and snorkeling have to do with unhurried leadership? Much is said about the importance of having a long-term vision of the work we are doing. We who lead need to see in our mind's eyes where we are going and what we are intending to do. Of course.

But these stories suggest that whatever vision *from* God we may have in our hearts and minds, it will be most rich, rooted, and creative when seen within a vision *of* God. Any holy vision from God is reflected light from our vision of God.

We need a vision of God that gives us leaders a sustainable vision for what we can do to serve God in our life and in our work, always in communion with him. Such a vision for serving God honors God's heart and purposes. It is the fruit of a growing vision of God in all his glory, goodness, beauty, and truth. The visible aims of our lives are the fruit of a vital and hidden root system.

SEEING GOD AT WORK

I'm a thinker. I take a lot of pleasure in dreaming about the future for my life, my family, and my work. I find it energizing to envision holy and good possibilities that, with God's guidance and empowering, I might be involved in. But I also find that I sometimes arrive at a vision of the future that seems to highlight my big part next to God's apparently small part in that vision. When that happens, I limit my view of God's ability to act in my life. God becomes the God of practical deism, his work being mostly historical rather than current, mostly universal rather than particular. But it is both God with us and God within our vision that will enliven our work. Jesus made it quite clear in John 15:5 that apart from him we can do nothing. We can be quite busy apart from him, but busyness and fruitfulness are not necessarily the same. What we as leaders therefore want to discover is the intersection of God's vision and ours.

The reason a vision *of* God is so important as the backdrop or foundation for our work is that we need to remember what—or, really, who—is truly good, and that is God alone. God wills good for me, for you, for his people, for his world. I get into trouble when I think that my efforts are the main cause of good rather than humbly welcoming good from God—directly or as a gift from others. A vision of unhurried influence grows out of a vision of God whose will is our best good. As we come to know and rely on the desirability of what God wishes for us, our vision of work is prompted by the goal of divine good and infused with holy energy.

However, when we do our work against the backdrop of a distorted image of God, then our lives, our relationships, and the work itself is also distorted. We become stuck in a life vision or work vision that grows, cancerlike, out of an internal image of God that isn't at all inviting, attractive, or—most importantly—true. We find ourselves seeking first a vision for our life or our work rather than seeking first a sense of being at home in God's good and beautiful purposes. A true vision of God as our source of strength and the only source of good opens our eyes to the genuine significance of our life and our work. Without that vision, we can tend to then overestimate the influence of what we do and—as a byproduct— underestimate the importance of who we *are*. We forget that in God's economy who we are nearly always trumps the influence of what we do. In *A Testament to Devotion*, Quaker professor Thomas Kelly put it this way:

> We Western peoples are apt to think our great problems are external, environmental. We are not skilled in the inner life, where the real roots of our problem lie. For I would suggest that the true explanation of the complexity of our program is an inner one, not an outer one. The outer distractions of our interests reflect an inner lack of integration of our own lives. We are trying to be several selves at once, without all our selves being organized by a single, mastering Life within us. Each of us tends to be, not a whole self, but a whole committee of selves.

Holding at the center of our lives and our work a compelling and holy vision of God unites our many activities around a God-focused center. We find that we can do our work from a place of integrity and peace. We can come to live the same life in public that we do in private. We can find holy focus in the midst of many demands, expectations, pressures, and opportunities.

Spiritual practices that enable us to welcome God's purposes with a humble and receptive posture do so much good in us—but we have to get a clear view of God in order for these practices to bring us close to him.

A LESSON FROM ISAIAH THE PROPHET

It was a year of political turmoil. A king had died after reigning for over fifty years. For the last ten, however, he was coregent with his son Jotham because of his prideful offering of incense in the temple that wasn't his to offer. In this tumultuous and uncertain time, the prophet Isaiah sought God's presence and was given a vision regarding a transition in Israel's leadership. When our situation becomes ambiguous and unclear, what we need first is not situational clarity but a fresh vision of God with us. This is the gift God gave Isaiah. As you read, try to imagine being in Isaiah's position:

> In the year that King Uzziah died, I saw the Lord, high and exalted, seated on a throne; and the train of his robe filled the temple. Above him were seraphim, each with six wings: With two wings they covered their faces, with two they covered their feet, and with two they were flying. And they were calling to one another:
>
> > "Holy, holy, holy is the LORD Almighty;
> > the whole earth is full of his glory."
>
> At the sound of their voices the doorposts and thresholds shook and the temple was filled with smoke. (Is 6:1-4)

Isaiah sees God enthroned and exalted high above him. The Lord's robe has a train that would make Princess Diana's wedding dress seem like a house dress. His train fills the whole temple, and majestic angels—seraphim—call humbly and beautifully to one another, "Holy, holy, holy is the LORD Almighty. The whole earth is full of his glory." It's not inconceivable that until this moment, Isaiah felt the whole earth was full of darkness and upheaval. How did Isaiah respond to this absolutely glorious vision of God?

> "Woe to me!" I cried. "I am ruined! For I am a man of unclean lips, and I live among a people of unclean lips, and my eyes have seen the King, the LORD Almighty."
>
> Then one of the seraphim flew to me with a live coal in his hand, which he had taken with tongs from the altar. With it he touched my mouth and said, "See, this has touched your lips; your guilt is taken away and your sin atoned for." (Is 6:5-7)

The weight of God's glory pressed down on Isaiah, and he felt woe rather than blessing. He saw himself and his shortcomings in the light of divine perfection. He felt dirty in the presence of such holiness. But God provided for Isaiah: one of the angels touched his lips with a refining coal from the altar of God. What was unclean was made clean—an unearned and undeserved gift. Sometimes rather than leaving us buoyant and bright, a vision of God causes us to feel our own mess, our own failure, our own shortsightedness. But God does not leave us there. God reaches down to us to take our guilt away. Just as Isaiah needed this, so do we.

And how did this vision of a glorious *and* merciful God affect Isaiah? What did this vision stir in him? When he heard God ask, "Whom shall I send?" Isaiah responded, "Here am I. Send me!" (6:8).

Isaiah's vision of God's presence made him aware of God's search for a spokesperson, an emissary, someone to speak for him. Blessed by a fresh sense of the gracious favor of the Lord, Isaiah didn't hesitate to speak up, seize the opportunity, and offer to do the Lord's work. Isaiah received a clear calling to serve God's purposes as, in his case, a prophet. Isaiah's calling was the direct fruit of his vision of God. His calling came *from* God. He saw God, he experienced the fullness of God's mercy and grace, and the result of this encounter was a calling to God's service. God continues to take these steps today to invite us into the companionship of ministry, whether that is a paid role or one we give freely to honor our God.

Later in his book, Isaiah reported these words from the Lord:

> Do not fear, for I am with you;
> > do not be dismayed, for I am your God.
> I will strengthen you and help you;
> > I will uphold you with my righteous right hand. (Is 41:10)

This sense of God's authorizing and empowering presence rested on Isaiah even many years later as he continued to serve God's purposes. Why was Isaiah able to live and work fearlessly? Because he remembered that he was never alone—and that the One who was with him and who is with us as our helper and upholder is Almighty God. Isaiah showed us with his life a God who strengthens us when we are weak, helps us when we can't do something alone, and upholds us when we are flagging, falling, or fallen.

A LESSON FROM PAUL THE PREACHER

Saul of Tarsus was a Jewish rising star in the days following Jesus' death and resurrection. A passionate Pharisee, he zealously followed God, even persecuting with murderous rage the followers of Jesus (Acts 9:1). What image of God filled Saul's heart and mind and fueled such a bloody, merciless campaign? Saul's God was passionately partial to the Jews, particularly those Jews who followed—as Saul did—a rigorously conservative interpretation of the Law and the Prophets. But Saul underwent a radical transformation when the resurrected Jesus himself challenged this vision of God. Saul's transformative journey to Damascus is a familiar story:

As he neared Damascus on his journey, suddenly a light from heaven flashed around him. He fell to the ground and heard a voice say to him, "Saul, Saul, why do you persecute me?"

"Who are you, Lord?" Saul asked.

"I am Jesus, whom you are persecuting," he replied. "Now get up and go into the city, and you will be told what you must do." (Acts 9:3-6)

The Jesus who Saul believed to be a false messiah and who therefore needed to be opposed with every ounce of his moral outrage became the Jesus who Saul saw as the Lord to be followed. Saul's initial vision of Jesus as an opponent of God prompted him to fight everything having to do with this rabbi from Nazareth. The corrected vision—this clear vision of God in Christ's face—transformed Saul to Paul, a lifelong fighter on behalf of his Jesus and the gospel.

Consider the outcome of Saul's dramatic encounter with Jesus: "The men traveling with Saul stood there speechless; they heard the sound but did not see anyone. Saul got up from the ground, but when he opened his eyes he could see nothing. So they led him by the hand into Damascus. For three days he was blind, and did not eat or drink anything" (Acts 9:7-9). Paul's vision of God made him temporarily blind. The man who had been the master of his fate and the fate of thousands was now utterly dependent and needy. Again, this profoundly humbling experience opened Paul's soul to reconsider and reconstruct his vision of God.

Many years later, Paul wrote to one of the many churches he had planted. In that letter to fellow Jesus-followers in Ephesus, Paul said that "we are what he has made us, created in Christ Jesus for good works, which God prepared beforehand to be our way of life" (Ephesians 2:10 NRSV). Paul had come to understand that all the good work Jesus Christ invited him to do was an expression of the gracious and creative hand of God working in his life. For Paul—and this is true for all of us—the work of God was first something God did in him, and then it became the good work Paul did for others. It is all too easy to get that sequence reversed, imagining that our good works come first and then God comes along behind to pick up the slack for what we might have missed.

A vision of God as the master and us as his work of art transforms our vision of whatever good work we might engage day to day. God is creative, good, wise, and mighty. What kind of work does such a God do? Creative, good, wise, and mighty work. He is doing that sort of work in us, and he is doing that sort of work through us as well.

Twenty years ago, I served on the staff of a Southern California church. We were being influenced by the best of the spiritual renewal that was happening through the ministry of the Vineyard Church. Our tradition had not included a lot of experience with visions, but we began to receive the gift of occasional visions from God at that time.

Once, when Gem and I were praying, she saw an image of a large tree floating in air. It was like a single scene from a movie. I found myself drawn to ask God if there was anything else he wanted to show us about this scene. As I prayed, the scene picked up from where it had left off and Gem saw the next scene. It was like watching a movie, having it pause, then seeing it unpause each time I prayed. This happened eight times. The pause-and-play vision went like this: Gem saw (1) a floating tree, rootless and fruitless, (2) send roots down and become grounded, (3) begin to bear fruit (4) that refreshed people sitting underneath. As they ate, they transformed into trees themselves, (5) spreading out in row upon row of trees extending out of view. (6) Then, she saw an aerial view of a large orchard continuing to expand, (7) until she saw an outline of the United States filling to the edges with rows of trees. (8) Then, yellow arrows beginning in the United States went up and over to other countries.

For a young couple who was currently serving in a small local church, it was a surprising vision. It seemed to speak of a future expansion of ministry. As we've reflected on this vision in the years since, we are grateful for ways we've seen it bear good fruit.

But one of the mistakes we sometimes made when thinking about this vision was that it was first about something we would do right away. We thought the vision was an immediate plan for action. In our case, something Oswald Chambers says in *My Utmost for His Highest* (in the July 6 reading) proved a sustaining and guiding insight while we waited to see what this vision would look like in reality. The title of that entry is, appropriately enough, "Visions Becoming Reality."

Chambers says,

> Every God-given vision will become real if we will only have patience. Just think of the enormous amount of free time God has! He is never in a hurry. Yet we are always in such a frantic hurry. While still in the light of the glory of the vision, we go right out to do things, but the vision is not yet real in us. God has to take us into the valley and put us through fires and floods to batter us into shape, until we get to the point where He can trust us with the reality of the vision. Ever since God gave us the vision, He has been at work. He is getting us into the shape of the goal He has for us, and yet over and over again we try to escape from the Sculptor's hand in an effort to batter ourselves into the shape of our own goal.

We assume that the next step after receiving a vision is to get moving and get working. But I've found that often God wants first to make the vision real in our actual lives so that we can live the vision and then see it realized through our work. This has required a lot of patience over the years. But it has borne fruit that encourages me and brings me deep joy.

And the vision wasn't just something personal. We've come to believe that it is an invitation God is extending to anyone who wishes to become people of growing influence. The first invitation is an invitation to become rooted—to abide. This is the path to fruitfulness of life, of relationships, of work. This is how lasting influence occurs. It is the fruit of deep abiding in Christ that serves and refreshes others. It is this fruit that reproduces itself in the lives of others. They then become fruitful so that this life can spread far beyond local impact.

MAKING TRUST THE ENGINE OF OUR WORK

I discovered that the best engine of my good work, of my initiative, and therefore of my leadership and influence is found in my assumptions about, my expectations of, and my vision of God. Sometimes this inner vision of God has been good, true, and beautiful, and the work I've done reflects this. But when my inner vision of God is distorted and unattractive, my work tends to be distorted and unattractive. Unfortunately, for example, I have done a lot of work driven by the engine of anxiety. That work had the smell of trying to control outcomes and other people. It was driven by a vision of a god who was far less involved or interested in my life than God actually is. How much better to work and serve powered by the engine of trust! An aroma of confidence and peace arises from trust in a God who has all the outcomes in his loving, caring hands. Trusting friendship with God through Jesus inspires, guides, and energizes truly fruitful work.

But what happens if Christians serving in business or in another public sector regard their lives as followers of Jesus as largely incidental to how they do their work? I'm not arguing for a more religious workplace. I am, however, suggesting that the resources we need to do good, productive, even profitable work in those arenas will come as we discern what it means in very practical terms to seek God's reign and God's good ways in our work life. It will come as we trust that in seeking God and his kingdom first, we will find what we actually need to work or lead well.

What do you need to do good work today? Creativity? Strategic insight? A uniting and compelling vision? A shared team spirit enabling well-coordinated efforts? Ideas for expanding business? A restored spirit in the midst of hard seasons in the work? And where will we find these? Will we look first at the latest business book, a new and popular conference, a business consultant or coach, team brainstorming, or something else? All of these are great resources, but what if we took advantage of them after we first sought God personally and, where fitting, as a group? What if we looked to God to see where he might lead us—and then if we still felt the need, turned to other resources? This is where my friend's one-third rule comes into play. We are wise to devote one-third of our planning time to the preparatory practices of spiritual, communal, or missional skills. Doing so is a practical way to both make seek-God-first opportunities a priority and to practice God's presence as we work.

Far from making us more religious in the negative sense of the word, we might, by God's grace, actually become more humbly confident, more insightful and creative, more strategically wise, a better team player, and so on. After all, we would have made our trust in God an engine of our work rather than something merely incidental to it. Those of us who claim to follow the most brilliant man who ever lived will find that he is quite a good source of all that we need to do our work as he might do it were he in our shoes.

When trust in God is the engine empowering our work, we may also find that our character and ethics are strengthened or perhaps even restored. When we enjoy a conversational relationship with God throughout the day, we may also see that we more naturally and winsomely share our faith with others. Our orientation to God being at the center of our work will enrich our spiritual journey, and a greater sense of God with us may increase our gratitude to him who enables us to do fruitful creative work beyond what is possible in our own strength.

Now, it's true that fear, anxiety, and other unholy engines can lead people to accomplish impressive things. But sustainable excellence is fueled by the commitment to serve God and by his life-giving joy in us. His eternal love in us and our trust in him will serve as a far better engine for good work than fear, anxiety, anger, or perfectionism will.

SPIRITUAL COMPETENCE, SPIRITUAL CONFIDENCE, EMPOWERING GRACE

What about the confidence that leaders need to influence people? What is a good engine for that? Not many people follow nervous, uncertain leaders, but where do effective leaders find confidence? Is it rooted in self-reliance and self-assurance, or is it fueled by a simple but consistent gaze on the faithful one? Spiritual leaders have a holy confidence that completes Christlike humility, gentleness, and patience. Anger, pride, and vanity contribute nothing to spiritual leadership that honors God and inspires people.

When we trust more in God than we do in our own opinion, perspective, or assessments, our vision of a kingdom way forward in our relationships and our work will be clearer. Our holy, humble confidence in God and, therefore, in the steps we take as leaders will grow. When our vision arises from our own judgments, opinions, and plans, however, we will at best see only a blurred connection between our leadership activities and the call to seek first God's kingdom in every aspect of our life. That observation may be rather unremarkable, but it points to a fundamental issue: Is my leadership and spiritual influence rooted in self-confidence or God-confidence? Do I know the difference between the two? God-confidence is the fruit of a sharply focused vision of God; self-confidence is tunnel vision for something I decide to accomplish for God—and of course I'll ask his blessing. That sounds a little sarcastic, but I've been guilty of that sort of tunnel vision too many times.

Since a discussion of God-confidence will be more worthwhile, consider what Paul said to the Corinthian church about such holy confidence: "Such confidence we have through Christ before God. Not that we are competent in ourselves to claim anything for ourselves, but our competence comes from God. He has made us competent as ministers of a new covenant—not of the letter but of the Spirit; for the letter kills, but the Spirit gives life" (2 Cor 3:4-6). Specifically what confidence was Paul talking about here?

In a letter that contains much in defense of his ministry, Paul says that his confidence is rooted in his relationship with God and with this faith community. The people themselves were sufficiently clear evidence that the Spirit had used Paul to write into their hearts good and new things that hadn't been there before. The sort of competence *this* kind of leadership requires is more than mere natural talents or charisma, more than human education or training, more than organizational leadership experience. All of those are God-given and therefore good gifts, and he will bless our exercise of them. But the competence Paul spoke of here is a relational and even spiritual competence.

Did, however, the very capable Saul, who went about persecuting followers of Jesus—did this Saul with all of his connections, education, passion, and abilities—have this kind of competence? I don't think so. But when Saul became Paul, his spiritual competence came from many years of his growing and deepening communion with God, in the solitude of the Arabian deserts or on the roads from town to town. Paul learned to discern the voice, the presence, and the heart of the Father, and this sensitivity made him competent for the kingdom work that he did so fruitfully. Paul didn't claim a competence that was rooted in himself. He acknowledged a competence that had been given him by God. It was an unearned, undeserved competence, and Paul exercised it with confidence.

This sort of holy confidence is born more out of willingness than willfulness. Holy confidence does not emerge from a bullheaded and self-assuming vision *for* God that defines some program, project, or human endeavor. Holy confidence springs from a rooted vision *of* God—of his person, presence, and desire and ability to work in me and through me.

PRACTICE: *ORA ET LABORA*

A while back, I saw the power of contemplation when I helped facilitate a leadership retreat at a nearby Benedictine abbey. There is something remarkable about a community of believers who have spent hours a day, day after day, month after month, decade after decade, prayerfully seeking God and resting in him. While I was there, I was reminded of one of the core values of the Benedictine tradition, artfully designed into a stained-glass window with the Latin words *ora et labora* written there, meaning "pray and work." Members of a Benedictine community live according to a rhythm of hours of prayer and hours of work. The ancient tradition was to rise in the very early hours for Vigils (a word drawn from the Latin for "wakefulness"), then retire for a bit until dawn when the community would greet the new day with Prime (the first hour of the day). They would begin their workday with Lauds, break midmorning for Terce (the third hour), stop midday for Sext (the sixth hour), break again midafternoon for None (the ninth hour), close their work day with Vespers (a word for evening), and then, just before retiring for bed, pray once more with Compline (a word related to the idea of completion). Today, only a few very rigorous Benedictine communities still practice all eight of these daily hours. It is far more common for there to be perhaps four hours of shared prayer: morning, midday, evening, and night.

These pauses in the midst of a workday are opportunities to remember and acknowledge God in the midst of one's daily labors. And it may seem that the rhythm is something like "work, then pray" or "pray, then work," but the idea is more integrative than that. Mother Teresa understood this. Once she was asked how they managed to keep up the demanding and draining work of caring for the dying poor in the dirty streets of Kolkata. Her answer was this: "We do our work for Jesus and with Jesus and to Jesus, and that's what keeps it simple. It's not a matter of praying sometimes and working others. We pray the work."

We pray the work, and we labor at prayer. Our work can have a heart of prayer, and our prayer can have hands that work with love. Contemplation gives birth to impactful work; good work grows in the soil of contemplation. They can't really be separated.

At a practical level, I find this idea of praying the work very freeing and energizing. I sometimes find myself overwhelmed by many tasks or projects or people needing my attention. When I'm at my best, I meet these concerns with prayer. A heart conversation with God in the midst of my busy day is an opportunity to focus my work, order it in terms of what matters most to God and to me, and engage the work fruitfully, peacefully, and with greater courage.

In the spirit of Mother Teresa, "We cannot all do great things, but we can all do small things with great love." What a helpful perspective when I am doing a lot of things that seem insignificant and small! I can do those little tasks with a heart full of God's love. I can pray with gratitude and trust for the person whose email I am answering. I can even remember the goodness of God as I work through a pile of paper sitting on my desk.

I love the simplicity that comes from being keenly focused on seeking God first. The vision of God that we gain by doing so gives us a clarity and singleness of purpose as we undertake the work he has entrusted to us. I pray that, together, we might continue to learn to set our hearts and minds on things above (Col 3:1-2) in the midst of everything we are doing. May we grow in our ability to focus on Jesus, the source and the reason for all our activities (Heb 12:2). And may we rejoice in the rich and lasting fruit God blesses us with as we focus our vision on him.

Unhurried Leadership Reflections

1. Take a few moments to imagine a road trip you've taken. Picture in your mind's eye the scenery around you whizzing by while the horizon remains stable. Ponder and then describe in your own

words what this image says about God's reliable presence in the midst of your many comings and goings.

2. If you can, listen to an audio version of Isaiah 6:1-8. (Youversion .com has audio Bible versions available.) As you listen, imagine yourself in Isaiah's place. What aspect of the vision is most striking to you? What act might the unavoidable sense of awe prompt you to take? What would your sense of impurity before a perfectly holy God compel you to do? See if you can feel the gratitude and joy of God's forgiveness, and then the energy and zeal of your renewed desire to serve him, his people, and his purposes. What is God saying to you through this passage today? For what specific leadership situation or challenge, if any, is this message particularly relevant? Enjoy lingering in this vision a bit. Let it draw you into prayer.

3. Thomas Kelly observed that we Western peoples tend to think the great problems of life are outside of us when the real roots of our problems lie within, where we are less experienced living and being. Do you agree or disagree? Why? Talk about engaging the ideas and feelings within you, what prompts that activity, and what results from it. If paying attention to thoughts or feelings within you feels somewhat foreign, is there some resistance preventing you from going there? What might that resistance be? What might help you overcome these hesitations? What is the first step you sense God inviting you to take?

FIVE

Questions That Unhurry Leaders

I RECENTLY EXPERIENCED THE MOST significant transition in my leadership life.

I had just become executive director of the nonprofit I'd been associated with for most of my adult ministry life. This community included close friends, key mentors, and spiritual fathers I'd been encouraged and blessed by in countless ways over the years. As part of our strategic planning, our board, our staff, and some key alumni were beginning to pray and dream about our future as an organization. It was as this process was coming to fruition that two good friends, who were helping us quarterback this process, asked me a critical question: "Do you feel called to stay with this ministry or to start your own ministry?" It may not sound especially profound, but it was a critical moment for me.

I had shared with these friends some of the new doors that were opening to me as a result of my writing. I had been assuming that I would step through these doors as part of my role in this long-time organizational home. But their question surfaced ways in which my heart had been moving in new directions without my being very aware of it yet. It was a hard question for them to ask because they weren't looking for me to leave. Their question opened to me the possibility that God was actually nudging me to take a step off a cliff into an abyss—to launch a new nonprofit that would become a home for these new opportunities. It felt like leaving my comfortable nest.

Rather than tell me something, these good friends asked me a question. That question became a seed of discernment that finally led me to leave and launch a new ministry: Unhurried Living.

Jesus was the master of asking good questions. Remember when four men lowered their paralyzed friend down through a roof to get him close to Jesus? Jesus asked those teachers of the law a couple of questions: "Why are you thinking these things? Which is easier: to say to this paralyzed man, 'Your sins are forgiven,' or to say, 'Get up, take your mat and walk'?" (Mk 2:8-9).

On another occasion Jesus was in a synagogue on the sabbath and saw a man "with a shriveled hand" in the congregation (Mk 3:1). Some of those present wanted to see whether Jesus would violate (their understanding of) the sabbath law and do the work of healing on that sacred day. Jesus asked the witnessing crowd a question: "Which is lawful on the Sabbath: to do good or to do evil, to save life or to kill?" (Mk 3:4).

These questions Jesus asked awaken me to my tendency to sometimes seek answers from Jesus for *my* questions but to fail to listen for *his* questions to me. If I feel I've received an answer to my question, I am tempted to take that answer and leave. When Jesus gives me a question, though, I find it keeps me a bit closer to him. Jesus seems to have a bias for doing things in a way that sustains and deepens our relationship with him.

As a follower of Jesus, Paul the apostle showed his mastery of using questions well in the many letters he wrote to churches. Among my favorite questions that Paul asked are five found in Romans 8:31-39.

More effectively than direct answers would, these questions touch me in a place where my soul needs to be reminded of deep truths.

UNFAILING FAVOR: GOD IS *FOR* US

Paul's first question is actually an introduction to the five key questions. He asks, "What, then, shall we say in response to these things?" Those "things" are the truths Paul had set forth in his letter, especially his comments in Romans 8 about the life the Father has made available to us through the Son—life empowered by the Spirit. Now Paul makes his points by asking bracing questions that, rather than inviting pat answers, provoke deep heart reflection.

The first of our five questions is simply, "If God is for us, who can be against us?" (Rom 8:31). It's a question that speaks to our experiences of outward opposition or perhaps even inward resistance to God's direction. It's a question that highlights anything that seems to be against us, anything opposed to the good that God intends for us. I'm glad Paul didn't ask only "Who can be against us?" For me, that would prompt a tidal wave of candidates real and imagined. Paul asked a bigger, better question when he began with "If God is for us" (and "if" here implies "since"). Paul's question puts everything that stands in opposition to us in the context of our omnipotent God's immeasurable grace. God is *for* us. He really is. Do you believe that truth in your heart of hearts? Does this statement of divine favor serve as the foundation of the whole of your life? Or do you feel somehow that God is, at best, ambivalent toward you or, worse, against you? Have certain circumstances tempted you to conclude that God couldn't possibly be for you? Paul's question is designed to expose such misguided and false assumptions.

It's remarkable how many Christian leaders have found themselves, in some blurry and ill-defined way, trying to earn God's favor or to prove their worth to him or parents or a spouse, or perhaps to themselves. But God already is for us. God desired our good before we realized what good was. God was working for our good before we took our first step. God is near us and involved in our lives and our hearts and is working for our good. If *that's* true, then who or what in this world could effectively stand against us?

God is not against me, and God is not against you.

God has done and is doing everything he can—and nothing is impossible for him—so that you and I might fully enjoy true life and deep joy because of our relationship with him. God is working so that we might be all that he means us to be in this world. God really is *for* us. Now, that truth doesn't mean that God is necessarily for our big ideas or our impressive plans or our personal projects. Some of these, instead of finding resonance with the Spirit and roots in God's kingdom purposes, might well be all about my own little kingdom: I sometimes have plans I think are for God that God himself is not for. Clearly, Paul was not saying that God is for us in that he takes our view of things or that he wants for us whatever we want for ourselves. Paul was saying that God sees us, knows us, and is *for* us for our good and his glory.

I have experienced the reality of God's gracious favor, of God's being for us, most deeply in my interactions with brothers and sisters in Christ who follow Jesus in the face of harsh persecution. As I write this chapter, I am a week away from visiting Christian leaders in Nigeria who I get to spend a few days with in retreat. Many of those leaders will travel to our meeting from parts of Nigeria that are under heavy attack by radical Muslim fundamentalists. Once when I was speaking to these fellow friends of Jesus, I asked how many in the room had lost a family member or close friend to martyrdom. Nearly every hand went up. Following Jesus puts them at risk for their lives. These brothers and sisters put themselves in great danger by following Jesus and serving his kingdom purposes. Yet in this reality where people are obviously and zealously against them, so many of these believers have a very simple and well-rooted trust that God really is for them. They know that with God for them, there is no one who can do them lasting harm.

Take a moment now to consider anything in your life that is against you. I just took a moment to sit in a comfortable chair in our backyard. It happens to be a cool morning, and I hear some very joyful birds telling the world how they feel. I sat down intending to let whatever feels against me surface in my thoughts and feelings, and then to answer those with the simple and powerful truth that God is for me. As I sat, I felt anxieties rise about upcoming speaking engagements, so I reminded myself, *But God is for me.* As I sat longer, some familiar insecurities and doubts came to mind. Again I said to my soul, *But God is for me.* For twenty minutes I let whatever has recently felt against me come to mind, and I simply remembered, *But God is for me.* Little by little, peace replaced anxiety; simple confidence replaced insecurity and doubt; a sense of being favored and loved replaced fear. If God is for me, who or what can really be against me?

UNFATHOMABLE GENEROSITY: GOD SPARES NOTHING

We come to Paul's second question, which flows naturally from the first. Just how do we know that God is for us? Paul's question suggests how: "He who did not spare his own Son, but gave him up for us all—how will he not also, along with him, graciously give us all things?" (Rom 8:32). God is not for us just in sentiment or mere words. God has already given us what is most precious: his own Son. This is more than a theological truth; it is a relational reality. The Father has given his Son so that we might be free of our sin and therefore free to enter into communion with God. That which is most priceless and precious is already ours.

Again, note that Paul didn't just ask, "What won't God give us?" Without the context of Paul's question, I might think of many things I don't deserve from God. But when Paul asked, "What won't God give us?" in the context of God already having generously given the gift of his own Son, Paul pointed to the truth that God's capacity for generosity is limitless. So what do I feel I need but don't seem to have access to? Do I feel anxious with no relief in sight? How will God *not* give me all the peace I need if I simply ask? Do I despair about my future due to personal shortcomings or situational impossibilities? How will God *not* be the God of all hope for me so that I might look to the future with genuine anticipation of what he will do? We can remind ourselves that every good is a lesser good than the gift of God's Son. Since God has given us Jesus, we can be absolutely confident that God will withhold nothing that would help us live in him, walk with him, serve him, and remain rooted in his kingdom.

Yet I find within myself a tendency to assume scarcity. Maybe it was being raised by a loving mother who spent most of her childhood in an orphanage where she experienced real scarcity. Maybe it was our simple family life growing up. For whatever reasons, I can tend to be a cup-half-empty person. Without the renewing work of the Spirit in my mind and heart, I would look at creation as a place where there is usually not enough for me. But Paul's question challenges that assumption. In fact, his question points to God's unfathomable generosity as evidenced in the invaluable gift of Jesus. Paul believed that as members of God's kingdom we have immeasurable resources to engage in his loving and good purposes for the world. It's not a generosity meant to merely fill my cup alone; it is a generosity that will overflow my life, leaving me full yet blessing anyone crossing my path.

So how does this truth of God's generosity and provision become practical for me in the day to day? With my predisposition to assume scarcity, I need to remember Paul's question and shine it on such thoughts and feelings. I lead a nonprofit ministry, and it's not uncommon to hit financially challenging seasons. (The same has been true in some church settings where I've served.) When I am privileged to teach, will I look only at these challenges and not at the biblical truth of God's overarching generosity to me in Jesus Christ as well as through the decades? Do I assume that the current challenges will last forever, or do I choose to trust in God's forever faithfulness? I make the truth of Paul's second question a truth for day-to-day life when I choose to trust that God's will meets me in a way I'll discover reflects his generous heart. When the immature thought fearfully whispers, "This season of shortfall will never end," I can ask that thought a question: "If my Father has not withheld from me his beloved Son, why would he withhold resources I need to live my life and do his work well?"

Now on plenty of occasions I have made a particular request to God that seemed to go unmet. How do I understand such seasons? I choose to believe that my generous heavenly Father is—in his infinite generosity—saying no so that he can say an even better yes in his good timing.

UNENDING JUSTIFICATION: GOD, MY DEFENDER

After prompting us to be awed by God's great generosity, Paul goes on to ask, "Who will bring any charge against those whom God has chosen?" (Rom 8:33). His qualifier is that it doesn't matter much who might seek to bring a charge against us since it is God who justifies. This third question and the fourth both unpack just how greatly "for us" God really is, especially in the face of whatever or whoever might stand against us.

Here Paul uses the metaphor of a prosecuting attorney bringing a charge against us in court. But God, Paul was communicating, will never put us on trial and then play the role of prosecuting attorney. God Almighty has instead chosen a relationship of speaking to us, providing for our justification, guiding us, and loving us: God is for us. Yes, the One who has unobstructed access to my most private thoughts could bring many charges against me. None of us, no matter how long we have journeyed with the Lord, has arrived at any sort of sinless perfection. We have, hopefully, learned at very practical levels the freedom of walking in God's forgiving ways and the emptiness of our wayward moments past. Also, just as guilty individuals who are on trial can be completely and safely honest with their defense attorney, I can be completely honest about my shortcomings and wrongdoings—about my sin—with the One who has chosen to defend me rather than prosecute me.

In light of my ongoing recovery from sinful habits, I am so grateful for the life-giving liturgy of confession we often say together in our Anglican church: "Most merciful God, we confess that we have sinned against you in thought, word, and deed, by what we have done, and by what we have left undone. We have not loved you with our whole heart; we have not loved our neighbor as ourselves. We are truly sorry, and we humbly repent. For the sake of your Son Jesus Christ, have mercy on us and forgive us; that we may delight in your will, and walk in your ways, to the glory of your Name. Amen." As I pray this prayer in community week by week, I am praying to the One who has chosen the role of my defender—and my God is the best defender around. No prosecuting attorney stands a chance against him in my case.

And that's an important truth because I actually do have an accuser, and so do you: Satan, who is called "the accuser of our brothers and sisters, who accuses them before our God day and night" (Rev 12:10). This accuser is continually bringing charges against us, and we give him plenty of material to work with. None of us is perfect. All of us have come up short, stumbled, struggled, even stepped over God's guiding line. All of us have sinned and continue to sin. This accuser is incessant, persistent, and determined to fill our hearts and minds with his accusations. But God is for us. God speaks as our defender, and—by his own choice—the resurrected Jesus stands at our side to support us. Who do you think will win this case? And to which voice will *we* listen? The voice of the just one, who has accepted us and welcomed us as his beloved? Or the voice of the one who stands against Jesus, and against us?

UNCEASING INTERCESSION: AN INSIDE ADVOCATE

Related to his third question, Paul asked a fourth question that moves beyond accusing and defending to condemning and interceding. The question is simply "Who then is the one who condemns?" Paul goes on to answer the question in some detail: "No one. Christ Jesus who died—more than that, who was raised to life—is at the right hand of God and is also interceding for us" (Rom 8:34). This question echoes the beginning of Romans 8: "There is now no condemnation for those who are in Christ Jesus, because through Christ Jesus the law of the Spirit who gives life has set you free from the law of sin and death" (Rom 8:1-2).

Paul's question reminds me that Jesus is seated at the right hand of God, a place of authority and favor. And from that position Jesus speaks with the Father and seeks my good. The center of reality here is that Father and Son converse not about condemnation but about promoting my true good. The Father—because of Jesus' death on the cross as payment for my sin—has decided the case in my favor. God has chosen me, forgiven me, and welcomed me into a relationship of love through Christ. Whoever would speak a word of condemnation about me will find that the judge does not give such a proposal any audience.

Speaking on similar themes, John the apostle encouraged his community by saying, "We have an advocate with the Father—Jesus Christ, the Righteous One. He is the atoning sacrifice for our sins, and not only for ours but also for the sins of the whole world" (1 Jn 2:1-2). Jesus is our advocate before the Father. So these third and fourth questions remind us that no accusation or condemnation will stick because God has chosen to favor us and accept us as cleansed of our sin because of Jesus' death and resurrection.

As an aside, I've found that we Christian leaders come with many different temperaments and tendencies. Some of us wrestle with a degree of arrogance while others are burdened by anxiety. Some of us are more tempted along the lines of self-promotion and others, of self-deprecation. But what all of us share is this focus on self: we look more steadily at ourselves than God. Paul's questions can draw our eyes away from our obsession with self to gaze at the One who is for us, generous with us, defending us, and interceding for our good. This brings us to Paul's last question—and my personal favorite.

UNCONDITIONAL LOVE: NEVER SEPARATED FROM GOD'S LOVE

Paul's last question reflects the greatest value in all of creation, the essence of God, and the guiding principle for all that he does. Paul asks, "Who shall separate us from the love of Christ?" He couples that question with another that suggests some possible causes of such a separation, namely, "trouble or hardship or persecution or famine or nakedness or danger or sword" (Rom 8:35). When our circumstances are troubling or hard, we may start to wonder about God's love for us. When we are attacked or when we don't have enough or when we feel threatened, we may doubt that God's love is actually unfailing. The longer I live and work in the arena of Christian leadership, the more convinced I am that this is a core issue for believers: Are we coming to know better, rely more fully on, and trust more completely the love God has for us (1 John 4:16)?

Acknowledging that we can frequently feel distanced from God and his love, Paul quotes Psalm 44:22 in Romans 8:36: "For your sake we face death all day long; we are considered as sheep to be slaughtered." Paul himself knew what it was to face death, to be a sheep led to slaughter. Troubles, hardships, and threats are not merely theoretical—and they weren't to Paul either. We experience tragedies and heartache, as do those we care about. May we choose in those moments to let the opposition, attack, trouble, or hardship point us to this Romans 8 truth that nothing can separate us from God's unshakeable love for us.

Will emotional low points separate me from God's faithful, unfailing love? Paul says, "No!" Will apparently insurmountable challenges distance me from God's real care and affection? Will inexplicable tragedy or unbearable heartache? No. In fact, Paul went on to say that God's ever-present love enables us to conquer and overcome these very opponents. God's love makes us strong. God's love makes us secure. God's love makes us confident. God's love restores our hope. There is nothing in the universe that has the power or ability to cause the smallest gap between us and God's measureless, reliable love revealed to us in Jesus (Rom 8:38-39).

Let me say a little more about this connection between suffering and love. It's common in my experience to hear people complain about their sufferings or hardships as evidence that God's love has somehow failed them. In contrast, twentieth-century spiritual director and theologian Friedrich von Hügel suggested that "suffering is the greatest teacher; the consecrated suffering of one soul teaches another. I think we have got all our values wrong, and suffering is the crown of life. Suffering and expansion, what a rich combination."

By God's grace there is indeed something redemptive and curative in the hard paths we travel. I think it is the consecration of our suffering that does it. Suffering alone is just pain. Suffering in the presence of a loving and faithful God, however, can drive our roots deeper into our knowledge and love for him than we imagined ever going. Suffering, for example, has awakened me from illusions that have captivated me and were driving me. Suffering has simplified my life. Suffering has reminded me that my life—my *real* life—is not defined by my activities, that what I accomplish is not the essence of my life. And suffering has slowed me down. Hurry has a way of making me skim the surface of God's loving presence in my life. Being slowed down by suffering gives me the opportunity to sink my roots deeper into my heavenly Father's love.

My own doubts about God's love for me gain traction and momentum when I gaze at my troubles instead of focusing my attention on who God is and what God has done in my life. Being in a hurry also affects my soul; again, I am distracted by the mounting circumstantial evidence that God's love has failed me here or there. I become focused on what troubles me or hinders me rather than on the One who is always with me and always loving me. The moment I lift my gaze and fix my eyes on Jesus, the moment I set my heart and mind on things above, the moment I remember spiritual reality—at that moment the God who is love changes everything.

What in your life tends to put distance between you and the Father's love? When, if ever, have you felt that the Father's love diminished at least a little bit because of something you've done or that he allowed another to do to you? How does the Father answer those nagging voices—"He would love me more if I . . ." or "He loves me less now that I . . ."? God reminds us, "There is nothing anywhere at any time that can get between you and me." May those words of truth transform our assumptions and our expectations.

Von Hügel also made another intriguing point about suffering:

> If we are Christians there are always two notes, suffering and joy. Gethsemane is awful, but it does not end with Gethsemane; there is the Resurrection. We want the whole of religion; renunciation and joy, the Cross and the Crown. I don't like Christians who have concentrated only on the Cross: Christianity is the whole life of Christ. His life of mortification, of suffering and sacrifice, culminating, it is true, in the Cross. But I can't bear the obliterating of his life, that great life lived, the touching humility and love.

Gethsemane is indeed awful, especially if it is my whole world. Wrestling with the apparent absence of God as you suffer is an exercise in meaninglessness. But, as von Hügel put it, Gethsemane is the precursor to the eventual resurrection, and that resurrection without Gethsemane and the cross makes no sense. I want to learn to say, with Paul the apostle, "I want to know Christ—yes, to know the power of his resurrection and participation in his sufferings, becoming like him in his death, and so, somehow, attaining to the resurrection from the dead" (Phil 3:10-11). I'm tempted to want only to know the power of his resurrection. To my earthbound ears, this sounds like a good deal. But the great commandment is not about power; it's about love. What Paul wanted most was not great power, but instead the great love Jesus exhibited as he hung on the cross. Paul wanted to be there with Jesus. He wanted to be close enough to Jesus to know his suffering and to share his own sufferings with him.

Again, Paul urges us to remember and trust that nothing—*nothing!*—can actually distance us from the active, engaged love of our heavenly Father.

PRACTICE: *GOD IS FOR ME*

If you didn't when you first read about it above, take a moment to try to see how God is for you in a relationship or situation that feels against you. After a while, thank God and praise him for how he is for you in every area of your life even when you don't see it and you struggle to believe it.

Unhurried Leadership Reflections

1. Think of a situation in your life, in a relationship, or in your work where you need something you don't yet have. As these come to mind, allow your heart to answer them with Paul's line, "But God did not spare his own Son for me." See what happens to your heart perspective as you engage this practice for a few minutes.

2. Personalize Paul's final question: "Who shall separate [your name] from the love of God?" First respond from the Father's perspective: "Nothing will be able to separate you, [name], from my love." Then, speaking to your heavenly Father, say with confidence: "Nothing in all creation will separate me from Your love." Allow these truths to be a place of reflection and meditation for a bit.

3. Think of those close to you—family, friends, colleagues. As each comes to mind, which of Paul's five questions do you think would prove most helpful to them right now? Pray that truth for them. Also consider how you might share this line of Scripture next time you're with them.

4. As you recall Paul's question reminding us that the gift of his only Son is the best argument for his continuing generosity to us, allow yourself to notice how God's generous grace has been present in your life over the last day or two. Look for little as well as big evidences of grace. Give God thanks as the Spirit brings these to mind.

SIX

Unhurried Influence

EXPLOSIONS ARE EXCITING. Who doesn't like a fireworks celebration at the end of a day at Disneyland or on the Fourth of July? The lake near our home hosts an annual Fourth of July fireworks display. When our boys were growing up, we would rise early that morning and put some camp chairs on the hillside overlooking the lake to reserve ourselves a place to enjoy. That evening, we'd sit as a family watching the whole sky light up as rocket after rocket exploded nearby. We could feel the impact of each explosion in our chests, and we went to a lot of trouble to get ourselves close enough to feel those fireworks.

In our leadership lives we also want an explosion of results from our efforts to serve the Almighty. But what if the work God wants to do in and through us was more like good fruit that will last? The fruit we buy at the grocery store rarely lasts longer than a week or so. Jesus, however, talked about fruit that will far outlast the excitement of an explosion (Jn 15:16)!

CHOOSING PEOPLE . . . AND SLOW-TO-APPEAR FRUIT

This kingdom fruit that lasts will, for one, be more people focused than thing focused. It is not uncommon for leaders to be interested in planning events, producing programs, or building structures. But events and programs that are amazing today likely won't be so amazing in a year or two. And although structures generally last longer than programs, buildings do not last as long as people do. People are eternal, so any work we do that directly helps people matters forever.

When my leadership was more event or program focused I would have said that everything I was doing did serve people. But looking back I see that my efforts were only indirectly for people. Most of my energy and focus were on making the *things* better rather than serving *people* better. This difference may seem subtle and insignificant, but people who have been led by both types of leaders have experienced the difference profoundly.

When I plan great events, produce amazing programs, and build impressive structures, I feel a sense of control over the variables that come into play. I can also feel a sense of accomplishment. But when I work specifically for people—serving them as they travel their unique and often bumpy journeys toward holiness and fruitfulness—I feel much less in control because I *have* less control, and the fruit of my efforts is far harder to assess by any short-term measurement. If my "fruit that will last" is only measured in terms of weeks, months, or quarterlies, I might not be contributing to kingdom longevity the way I could or should be.

In Southern California, where I've lived most of my adult life, many developers planted fast-growing varieties of eucalyptus in new housing developments because they wanted full-grown trees as soon as possible. But in many areas today, I see eucalyptus trees being torn down because they can be messy when they drop their leaves, dangerous when large branches are blown down by strong winds, and not very attractive. The developers' tree-planting approach bore much fruit in terms of giving neighborhoods big trees fast, but if you have to tear the trees down after only twenty or thirty years, it's not exactly "fruit that will last." Compare the eucalyptus to a California redwood forest where the age of those trees is measured in centuries. I want to be building people who will keep growing for decades, even generations, rather than planning events, programs, and structures that will eventually be worn down or torn down.

We can, however, find it difficult to invest time and effort in fruit that doesn't appear quickly; it's hard to wait to see if your work was effective. Consider the task of training others to do something we already know how to do well. That investment of time is always less productive in the short term, but it will have an exponential impact in the long run. This idea isn't hard to understand, but many of us still struggle to invest time in training others because the fruit will be a long time coming. But over time reproduction—teaching someone to fish—will bear far greater and longer-lasting fruit than production—giving someone a fish you caught. Working with people to help them become followers of Jesus in their own Monday-to-Friday lives empowers them for a lifetime of personal transformation even after our time with them ends.

So how do we become the sort of people who reliably bear fruit that lasts? We improve the health, the wholeness, and the holiness of our inner life.

APPEARANCE VS. REALITY

Despite Jesus' concern about the internal, too many Christian leadership strategies for spiritual growth seem to focus on outward behavior and appearance. That focus seems to achieve quicker measurable results. As a leader, I have resisted coming clean about places of brokenness and unhealthy and unholy patterns because I want others to see me not as a struggler but as a conqueror. After all, that kind of exterior looks good to others, whereas the reality of my unchanged heart wouldn't. Again,

I write from experience: I tried to resolve my struggle on my own, but it didn't work. Jesus invites us to reveal our struggles. Somewhere near us God has provided a trusted friend in whom we can confide. That is a crucial first step in addressing our brokenness or emptiness.

When Christians fail to be honest about our struggles, those who follow us make the assumption that we are struggle-free, unlike them, and that they cannot follow such a perfect leader. How it would encourage followers to learn that their leaders are models not of perfection but (hopefully) of progress in spiritual growth.

That knowledge can sometimes puff us up (1 Cor 8:1) rather than form us should cause us to wonder about the assumption in our culture that education is the answer to everything. For example, some in the church believe that growing in biblical, doctrinal, or theological knowledge is an effective preventative to sin. But is it? First-century Jewish leaders managed to couple broad biblical knowledge with deep sins of the heart. There is a knowledge that runs deeper than merely knowing ideas or concepts. Loving knowledge of God is something God's Spirit wishes to cultivate in our lives. We must never overvalue knowledge *about* God and undervalue the loving knowledge *of* God.

Consequently, there is temptation to oversimplify when it comes to how we think about helping others grow. We settle for delivering more knowledge or urging more involvement in church programs: we focus on the external. But spiritual growth is both simpler and more complex than that. It is as simple and as challenging as following Jesus, walking with him and working with him moment by moment. And it's more complex than we can manage on our own. We need God's help and the friendship of others.

JESUS, THE TRUE VINE

I love the biblical image of Jesus as the true vine and me as a branch being nourished by that vine (Jn 15:1-8). That Jesus is the true vine, however, implies the existence of false vines that I might turn to in an attempt to get what I need. But only the true vine brings real life; a false vine might instead suck the life out of me completely. For example, we may seek to abide in our work life to draw out a sense of meaning and vitality. Good work is a gracious gift from the Father, but like any divine gift, our work can be made an idol and end up a false vine.

Jesus' metaphor helps me grow in the life of God by enabling me to identify the false vines I turn to in quest of what I need in my life. I can live knowing that Jesus alone is the true vine, that our Father in heaven is the true gardener in my life, and that I'm a branch who finds life only in abiding in the life-giving vine. This abiding produces abundant and lasting fruit in my life and work.

Despite my knowledge of the true vine and my relationship with him, sometimes I still try to find life in a false vine. I choose to abide in a false sense of control in order to reduce the anxiety I'm feeling or to abide in my too-familiar perfectionism in an effort to minimize the unpredictables in my leadership environment. But unpredictability is a human reality.

Or I will start trying to control certain outcomes so that I can know peace. With that decision I've already surrendered the deeper peace I have access to in my friendship with a reliable Savior. I am seeking to find peace in a well-managed system rather than in the Prince of Peace, whose peace could flow through me to bless others. When my plans don't turn out the way I had envisioned, I feel as if that peace has been stolen from me.

I have also chosen a false vine when I seek to satisfy my thirst for recognition with the acceptance and affirmation of other people. For instance, when I plan a big event and not enough people come, I feel empty and therefore angry at those I expected to be there. I feel ripped off because the recognition I was looking for and counting on is not going to come to me. I sought some sense of fullness and satisfaction by doing hard work that others would praise. The better option, however, is to abide in the true vine and discover that his recognition is all I actually need. When I choose to abide in the true vine, God can use me to point the way to Jesus rather than merely draw attention to myself. When I abide in the true vine, I am able to lead from a place of already being accepted and recognized by my Lord, who died on the cross for me.

My friend Chuck Miller shared a simple illustration that always helps me with this. The image involves a pitcher, a cup, a saucer, and a plate. Picture the cup on the saucer and both sitting on the plate. In the pitcher is all that God is and wants to pour into the cup, which represents my life. As God pours into me until I am full, the overflow spills out onto the saucer that supports me: the saucer represents all the relationships in my life. As God's people in my community receive all that God pours into our shared life, that overflow spills onto the plate, which represents the work of God we share.

Unhurried leadership gives sufficient attention to the process whereby God fills me to overflowing; it is the fruit of overflow rather than pouring out the last few drops of whatever we have on our own to give. When we are unhurried leaders abiding in the true vine, we lead from divine fullness in order to bless the emptiness around us rather than leading from emptiness as we look for fullness somewhere other than in the One who is life.

MAKING A TREE GOOD

For me, another especially meaningful metaphor that Jesus used in his teaching is the idea of making a tree good, and it will bear good fruit. In Luke 6, Jesus said that no good tree bears bad fruit. But what do we do to become that good tree, to come to places of wholeness, abundance, holiness so that our life is good and fruitful? "A good man brings good things out of the good stored up in his heart" (Lk 6:45).

In another place, Jesus said something similar:

> Make a tree good and its fruit will be good, or make a tree bad
> and its fruit will be bad, for a tree is recognized by its fruit. You

brood of vipers, how can you who are evil say anything good? For the mouth speaks what the heart is full of. A good man brings good things out of the good stored up in him, and an evil man brings evil things out of the evil stored up in him. (Mt 12:33-35)

These words come from conversations Jesus had either with or about the Pharisees. They elevated obeying the law above developing and nourishing relationships. Their concern about the law had them focused more on regulating behaviors. They preferred managing rules over tending relationships, which made them antagonistic toward Jesus.

What was Jesus' concern about those Pharisees? He called them whitewashed tombs because they looked the part of a godly leader on the outside, but the tree of their lives bore only bad fruit: they were proud, self-promoting, and self-righteous. Pride like that settles for making the tree look good rather than actually being good.

In order to look good, the Pharisees carefully drew lines around hundreds of God's commands in an attempt to be sure they would not break those laws. They were absorbed with the micro-commandments they had crafted and therefore missed the greatest commandment of all. God wants us first to love him with all that we are and all that we have, and then to be moved by that love to bless our neighbor with it (Mt 22:36-40). The Pharisees had lost touch with the center of their faith; instead they were engrossed in perimeter observances that were far less important and had far less an impact than nurturing our relationship with God does.

A GOOD TREE BEARING GOOD FRUIT

The Pharisees were masters of cultivating what some have called a false self. Many leaders have taken the same tack: we learn how to look a certain way in certain environments. We think, *This kind of person wins, so I'll become that kind of person.* But there is absolutely no better self for your leadership role than your true self. Jesus wants to make you—God's unique and treasured creation—into a good tree so you'll bear good fruit. The tree of who you actually are is the most fruitful you that you can possibly be.

In the short term, a false self may appear the more fruitful option. But God made us unique. No one else can do what I can or you can to honor and build God's kingdom, to embody some aspect of the Father's character. Making the tree good is about fully becoming our true self. Then we will produce good fruit that lasts.

The path to becoming a tree that produces lasting fruit may not be what we expect. I have a friend who is a farmer who often consults for other farmers in California's Central Valley about how to improve the health and increase the productivity of their crops. One time a large almond grower contacted him. Concerned about his trees, he asked my friend to visit. My friend told me, "When I looked at his orchard, I said, 'You haven't been pruning these trees well enough. They aren't going to last you more than a few more years unless you do. If you prune them really well this season, your productivity is going to go down significantly in the short term, but these trees will live a lot longer and produce a lot more in the long term.'"

Not able to see past those few years of low productivity, this farmer didn't take my friend's advice—and his trees only produced for a few more years. The substance of my friend's counsel was basically "Make the tree good," but the farmer could only see the immediate loss that would come if he followed that advice. He was afraid the cost of making the tree good was too high, when in fact making the tree good would have meant years of productive farming rather than ownership of, essentially, acres of firewood.

In terms of becoming a good tree in the spiritual sense, it helps to ask, "In what way was Jesus' own life a good tree?" In the Gospels, Jesus said, "I have come down from heaven not to do my will but to do the will of him who sent me" (Jn 6:38). Jesus lovingly and humbly surrendered his will to the wishes of his Father. That means, for instance, that

Jesus saw the crowds with compassion, as harassed and helpless sheep without a shepherd (Mt 9:36). That submission also means that he did not come to be served but to serve and give his life as a ransom for many (Mt 20:28). Jesus' leadership was gentle and humble of heart, prompting me to ask myself how much of my leadership has been rough and proud of heart. In our North American context, pride and pushiness are almost seen as leadership virtues. But the way of Jesus is different. Jesus lived as a good tree bearing good fruit, giving us an example so that we might to do the same.

WHEN BAD TREES TRY TO BEAR GOOD FRUIT

Many times in my own leadership experience, I've seen something about my life that wasn't healthy and whole. But instead of doing the hard work of making the tree good, I continued to manage appearances and stay busy with what I claimed was God's work. I focused all my energy and time doing work that was *out there* rather than giving necessary attention to what needed to be done *in me*. During those seasons I could have yielded to the rule and guidance of God's gracious hand, so that what flowed from within me would have been the life of God's Spirit. I could have actually experienced the heart transformation that results in the lasting fruit of godly influence. But sometimes I chose differently.

How do we deal with the temptation to make those poorer choices, yielding to sin rather than to the Lord? How do we, for instance, deal with lust? Some Christian leaders struggle and fall to the temptation to view pornographic images on their computers. A common strategy is to install a filter that will block such images. That's a perfectly good idea, though no filter yet exists that can completely block every inappropriate image on the Internet. So we need to ask: *Why do I want to go to those sites? What hurt am I trying to comfort? What need am I trying to meet?*

How about the temptation to anger? I am most often tempted to lose my temper on the Southern California freeways. Other drivers seem to trigger a sense of injustice in me. Sometimes I feel like I'm reacting not just to the driving situation but also to injustices I experienced in my youth. But what if I were able to see the person cutting me off differently, not as someone one who annoys me but as a person who knows hurt, if not brokenness and unhappiness? Could I choose to become more like Jesus and treat well those who mistreat me? Could I make the tree of my heart good in that way? To do so, I need to consider why I so easily lose my temper in these situations, whether these circumstances touch on a wound from the past that I haven't yet forgiven and released. What if I trusted more fully that I am perfectly safe living under the reign of Jesus?

One way I choose my path of leadership instead of God's is by trying to fill my need for recognition. As I've mentioned, too often my leadership has been about trying to meet my own needs in the name of doing something for the good of others. I focus on that outward good, but my inner motivation is to get attention. I lead out of a functional deism (as the author Parker Palmer has named it): whatever I do and however I do it, I am largely unaware of God's gracious, abundant, and engaged presence with me.

An example of how I've served in order to receive what I needed is my decision as a young adult to choose pastoral ministry as my vocational path. One of the motivations for that was that Jesus had dramatically changed my life for the better, and I found that experience easy to share with others. When I realized that I could have a job where this was one of my main activities, I jumped in with both feet. My decision didn't involve a high school guidance counselor or any standardized test. It was a matter of the heart for me. My genuine love for Jesus was what drove me into this work.

But right alongside that motivation was another that was far less pure. In the family I grew up in, we were not always good at affirming one another. So when I was growing up, I spent a lot of time trying to do well in school, get better on my guitar, or perform in a number of other ways, hoping to receive some recognition. Then, when I became a Christian and started attending a church that held the knowledge and teaching of Scripture in very high regard, it didn't take me long to see that studying God's Word and sharing what I learned was a quick path to mega-recognition. Every time someone affirmed an insight I shared, it was like crack cocaine for my recognition-starved soul. Seeking to quench my thirst for recognition, I brought that to my leadership role. Bad idea.

In practical terms, the problem surfaced when I began to realize that seeking to quench my thirst for recognition in the context of my leadership role didn't fully satisfy me. Leadership accomplishments and people's affirmation weren't quite enough. I was still thirsty. As I type those words, I hear what Jesus cried out in the temple courts: "Let anyone who is thirsty come to me and drink. Whoever believes in me, as Scripture has said, rivers of living water will flow from within them" (Jn 7:37-38). I should have taken my thirst for recognition to Jesus, but instead I took that thirst to my leadership roles and my relationships. I served in an attempt to get something I needed.

Taking my thirst to Jesus, however, would have led me to places where rivers of living water could flow from within me and bless those I served. Taking my thirst to my leadership role blocked that flow and left me thirsty. Recognition from others is not nearly as satisfying as hearing the Father speak to my spirit his words to the Son: "You are my Son, whom I love; with you I am well pleased" (Lk 3:22). When I heard those words of recognition, I started to be filled with divine affirmation, and my soul began to overflow with loving affirmation for others. When my soul was thirsty for recognition, I found it hard to affirm others—unless, of course, I was affirming others in order to get some affirmation from them.

In addition, if I keep taking my thirst for recognition to those I speak to or teach or shepherd, how willing will I be to give them a message that's hard to hear? It's not going to happen. Speaking hard truth even in love would jeopardize my human source of recognition. It's very hard to lead people from whom you desperately need something.

ACTUALLY MAKING THE TREE GOOD

Twenty-five years ago I began a journey of integrating spiritual formation and leadership development. At the time my vision of spiritual formation was thin, if not completely nonexistent, and my vision of leadership development was a strange brew of selfish ambition, anxiety, control, and hyperactivity. Even though I was a pastor, I seemed to leave behind whatever good there was in my communion with Jesus when it came time to engage in what I saw as the activities of leadership. It was as though I wore one suit of clothes when I was alone with God, praying, reading the Scriptures, or somehow engaging personally with him. Then I put on a completely different set of clothes—work clothes, if you will—when it came time to plan and implement programs, prepare and present messages, meet with and counsel people, and so on. My communion with Jesus and my acts of service were like two unrelated islands in my life.

By God's grace, I learned some practical steps for making the tree good. One of those practices has been enjoying unhurried time with God in solitude and silence. Wayne Anderson, a mentor, introduced many of us to this discipline, which he called "extended personal communion with God" and I've come to call unhurried time with God. He urged us to set aside the better part of a day once a month to simply be alone with God for no other reason than to be in God's presence, listen for his voice, and enjoy him in a peaceful, unhurried way. How this practice became a regular part of Wayne's life is an interesting story.

After having been active in a thriving ministry to students in Boston at the height of the Jesus People movement, Wayne planted a church in the city's western suburbs. He served there for six years, and at that point he found himself on the edge of burnout. Leadership felt draining.

He had lost any sense of the presence of Jesus with him. Yet Wayne felt he needed to keep leading the church, so he continued doing the right things on the outside while he was dying on the inside. In that dark place, God used Henri Nouwen's *The Way of the Heart* to bring some light. In that book, Nouwen talks about solitude, silence, and prayer, about waiting on God, and about being in the presence of Jesus.

Wayne realized that, although he had been a Christian for twenty years, he had never really taken time to be with Jesus, to simply listen to see if he would speak. Of course Wayne had led seminars and workshops on how to have a quiet time, but those were basically about studying the Bible and trying to apply the lessons of Scripture to life. So Wayne began an experiment: he took blocks of time—two, three, maybe four hours—to just be in the presence of Jesus. Wayne didn't try to get an answer to a question, a creative idea, or even a plan to do something exciting for God. He was just trying to respond in obedience to this simple but most challenging invitation: "Be still and know that I am God" (Ps 46:10).

As Wayne continued to be intentional about spending time with the Lord, Jesus began to speak to him and teach him. There was only one problem: Wayne didn't like what he was hearing. The message seemed to be, "Wayne, I want you to leave your church and spend a year alone with me." And what was Wayne's first response? "That's the craziest thing I've ever heard in my life! Let's talk about something else, Jesus." Yet in those regular times Wayne spent alone with God, this idea kept coming back. Wayne argued, "Leave my church? I'm the founding pastor. How will they get along without me?" (By the way, the church is still going strong decades after Wayne's departure. No problem there!) Wayne continued to wrestle with the idea: "Spend a *year* alone with Jesus? I have a hard enough time spending an *hour* alone with Jesus. And taking a year off from work? I'll eat up all of my savings. And what if I can't get a job at the end of that year off? I don't want to become homeless!"

After arguing with God for months, Wayne finally realized he had to either obey or stop listening to God. So he resigned. Wayne preached his last sermon on the last Sunday of July and the next week, filled his car with all his earthly belongings and headed across the country to Southern California. (Single all his life, Wayne was more easily able to pick up and move.)

That year was a truly transformational experience for Wayne. He walked the beaches of Laguna Beach and spent time praying, journaling, reading, and simply focusing on the very real presence of Christ with him. A primary fruit of that year was a fresh vision of what the Christian life is all about. Wayne's basic beliefs about God didn't change, but his experience of God made all the difference.

I am one of the many beneficiaries of the way of life Jesus cultivated in Wayne. His approach to leadership profoundly affected mine. In my own practice of stepping away regularly to be in God's presence, I often will come to that day in my schedule and think, "I cannot *possibly* step away right now in view of everything that needs my attention." But I cannot point to a single time in twenty-five years when, however busy the season, I stepped away to be alone for a few hours or even a whole day with God and then regretted it! And I *can* clearly remember countless times when God blessed me with creative ideas, necessary insights, or wise solutions that resulted in far more fruitful leadership than I would have been able to offer without that time away in Jesus' presence.

A VERY GOOD TREE THAT BORE VERY GOOD FRUIT

Make the tree good. That's an invitation, in part, to be unhurried in our efforts to have a lasting influence as we lead God's people. First, we leaders ourselves—all our activities and relationships, our plans and words—can be influenced by Jesus' presence with us and within us. Often we experience God's presence in a powerful way when we are with someone who loves him and has walked with him for decades. I experienced that kind of encouraging influence whenever I had a chance to be with Dallas Willard.

During his graveside service, I experienced a moment that is indelibly etched in my memory and that often comes to mind and inspires me. Across from me stood spiritual leaders who, like me, had been mentored by Dallas's life and his writings: he had modeled for us a kingdom way of living and leading. At one point each of us was given a rose to place on the coffin. As I laid my rose down, I didn't think about a talk I'd heard Dallas give, one of his books that I'd read, or an amazing insight I'd gained from his teachings. I found myself remembering the kind of person he was. I didn't think of his accomplishments, but of his manner, his character. The prayer that bubbled up within me was "Jesus, I would love to be the kind of person Dallas has been."

Dallas Willard was a very good tree. I long to be the kind of tree that bears very good fruit—fruit that lasts more than a week or a month, but for a year, for a decade, for eternity.

PRACTICE: *THE EMPTY CUP*

Think of your own roles, relationships, or activities of influence. When, if ever, have you entered into those places with an empty cup, seeking something to fill it? What were you looking for? Consider the truth that Jesus wants to fill your cup so full that you will have extra to share with the people you serve. What might he do to accomplish that in you? What might you do to cooperate with his work?

Unhurried Leadership Reflections

1. When you read about Wayne's experiment of spending a year alone with God, what do you think? What do you feel? How might Jesus be inviting you into a similar season alone with him, even if on a scale of hours or days rather than weeks or months?

2. Look back over places where you have opportunity to be an influencer in your life. See if you can identify a moment or an event that was very exciting and apparently fruitful but that now seems less impactful than you thought it was then. If you had an opportunity to go back and do something differently, what might that be? As you think about that situation, what does the invitation to "Make the tree good" say to you?

3. Think about a place of temptation that seems to be a continual struggle. In what ways are you tempted to hide that dynamic in your life? What might it look like to talk with a trusted friend about the struggle? How might you pour out your heart to God about any feelings of powerlessness, hopelessness or frustration about this temptation? Let this be a place of conversation with a God who already knows, understands, and cares.

SEVEN

How Grace Empowers Leadership

WHEN I WAS A RELATIVELY NEW follower of Jesus, I imagined reaching some point of maturity where I could say, "The days of my needing grace are long past. I have now arrived." I was painfully aware of what a mess I had made in my life without Christ, and I couldn't wait for that moment when I would get my act together. My awareness of my great need for grace was miniscule next to my awareness today, and that may be true for you as well.

What I have learned along the way is that grace is more than the starting point—it is a way to live and lead.

My mentor and friend Wayne Anderson once spent months studying the language of grace in the New Testament. He found more than 120 occurrences of the word in the English translation he was using. After reviewing every one of these references in their context, he found that far and away the majority of times the word *grace* was used, it wasn't referring to the free gift of salvation we receive by faith (a primary understanding of grace in many Protestant circles). Instead, *grace* most often referred to some facet of actually living out a

Christian life. Wayne used to say, "Just as I am saved by grace, so I live by grace, serve by grace, and lead by grace."

So where do I need grace in my life? When I'm honest with myself, I realize that I need grace in places where I am weak. I need the grace of patience where I'm so easily tempted to lose my temper when wronged. I need the grace of self-control where I'm tempted to self-indulgence. I need the grace of forgiveness when I stumble and fall. These are all gifts, manifestations of God's grace that he wants to give me and that I need.

BECOMING STRONG IN GRACE

Paul's invitation to Timothy was "You then, my son, be strong in the grace that is in Christ Jesus" (2 Tim 2:1). How does this work? How do I actually become strong in grace? The tense of the Greek "be strong" communicates that we are invited to be continually strengthened in the generous grace of Jesus.

My growth in grace has come as I've recognized where in my life I need grace and then acknowledged the presence of God's grace there. I have an amazing capacity to highlight what I see as my strengths and adopt a stance of "I don't need anything" or "I am self-sufficient" rather than noticing and addressing where I genuinely need forgiving grace, healing grace, empowering grace. And this grace is fully and freely available to me if I don't refuse it out of misguided pride or self-imposed blindness.

I have also realized that my human strengths can sometimes be a hindrance to kingdom progress. And I sometimes imagine Paul's words in 2 Corinthians 12:10 rewritten as "When *I* am strong, *he* is strong." Don't we sometimes interpret our apparent strength as a leader as evidence of God's strong presence within us? Of course God has given us strengths. He blesses our strengths and uses our strengths. But we get attached to our strengths and they become idols: our strengths become God replacements and, as such, can become lord instead of Jesus. We can easily start to rely on our strengths and depend on them in a way that is opposed to wise counsel like "Trust GOD from the bottom of your heart; don't try to figure everything out on your own. Listen for GOD's voice in everything you do, everywhere you go; he's the one who will keep you on track" (Prov 3:5-6 *The Message*). I don't want my strengths to distance me from God or turn me away from him. Instead, I want my wise and loving God to use my strengths to move me along his way for me.

Yet God has bigger purposes for our strengths and especially for our weaknesses. We are tempted to think that our greatest resource for life's demands is our strengths, but when it comes to following Jesus, it might be that our weakness is our greatest resource. That's because our weaknesses can prompt us to turn to him and rely on his guidance and power for whatever he has called us to do. To illustrate this, Jesus takes an image from a vineyard (Jn 15:4-6); a branch drawing on the sap of the vine is a picture of *dependent* strength. That stands in sharp contrast to the world's ideal of independent strength.

I have noticed a connection between my areas of influence and grace: when my vision of leadership is more hurried, that pace tends to indicate that I'm serving out of my own strength rather than relying on graced-by-God strengths perfected in my weaknesses.

LEADING AND WEAKNESS

During those times when we serve only out of our strengths, God will often teach us that we are not to depend on our strengths, but on the God who gives us those strengths. In God's leadership design, his cause is best served not when we are strong, but when his power fills us in our weakness. After all, when we feel weak, we usually feel dependent. And that is a very good place for learning to abide in God more completely and rely on his strength more fully.

Let me say here that I don't like feeling weak, looking weak, or being weak. I like looking strong and feeling strong. I want people to think I've got everything together, whatever that actually means.

Yet I have found that sharing only my strengths with those I lead or influence often discourages them rather than empowers them. We are all much weaker than we usually appear, much less admit, to the people around us. And so many of those people are profoundly aware of their own weaknesses, but they see only a leader's strengths and assume that there's no way for them to follow that example. Their leader can seem so far ahead that they'll never catch up. But I have yet to meet a Christian leader who does not have his or her own set of weaknesses. But too many leaders seem to believe that they should only speak of their strengths, never their weaknesses. The assumption seems to be that people will be discouraged to discover that their leaders at times stumble or struggle. It's strange that Christian leaders think they are supposed to be examples of perfection rather than of growth in their faith.

Now we come to a passage that has been a place of both challenge and wise counsel for me as I've been learning how grace works in leadership. In 2 Corinthians 12, Paul tells of his journey of spiritual transformation, and it doesn't appear that the transformation took years to unfold. But there came a point when he moved from a strong experience of God's presence to an experience of unanswered prayers and God's apparent absence. Paul went from feeling strong to feeling weak, but as he explains, that experience moved him toward real strength, kingdom strength. Some key insights from this passage have shaped me as a leader.

"STRONG" ENCOUNTERS WITH GOD

In the first half-dozen verses, Paul describes "a man in Christ" who experiences amazing visions and revelations from God. When this man is in God's presence, he hears things that he can't even speak about. About such a man Paul says he'd gladly boast, but he doesn't want to boast about himself unless he is boasting about his weaknesses (v. 5). Yes, this man is Paul, though he prefers not to speak too proudly about these remarkable experiences. Paul has had what we might call strong experiences of God's presence.

Let me clarify that Paul wasn't downplaying his résumé. Elsewhere, he speaks of his remarkable heritage as a Jew's Jew, his passion and discipline as a model Pharisee, and his zeal for the Jewish faith. If anyone had lived up to the demands of the law, Paul had (Phil 3:4-6). Clearly there wasn't much space or felt need for grace in Paul's life at that time. His story in 2 Corinthians 12, however, shows that this changes.

What parallels to these "strong" experiences of God do you see in your own life and leadership? Perhaps you think of seasons when your faith in Jesus meant peace and contentment, when God clearly answered your prayers, perhaps when you experienced God's presence, guidance, or voice in dramatic ways. Perhaps God blessed you with a season of visible ministry success. Maybe you had an experience of felt blessing or a moment of empowered service. Such experiences seem the sort of thing Paul is speaking of here, perhaps on a grander scale. What Paul calls "surpassingly great revelations" (v. 7) refers to moments when we see into spiritual reality in a way that amazes, surprises, or even terrifies us.

In my own experience, I think of moments early in my journey with Jesus. When I was a teen and young adult alone with my Bible, the Scriptures sometimes seemed to open the heavens to me. At times the reality of Jesus with me overwhelmed me. I couldn't get enough time reading and studying God's Word.

Later, after a season of draining ministry had transformed my vision of Jesus from friend and good shepherd to distant, demanding boss, God blessed me with mentors who reintroduced me to Jesus. God met me in moments of rediscovery as I practiced solitude, silence, and listening prayer, and those moments still shape me today. So do those precious times when simple truths of Scripture came alive for me in ways they weren't before. I also felt God's presence when I got a taste of Paul's being caught up into the heavenly presence of God. I think of seasons when God especially blessed our ministry to college students; what a joy to see that these dear individuals are still bearing fruit for the Lord decades later.

A SUFFERING CLOSE TO HOME

Paul goes on to say that "in order to keep me from becoming conceited, I was given a thorn in my flesh, a messenger of Satan, to torment me" (2 Cor 12:7). Paul admits that his remarkable visions and experiences of God tempted him to think more highly of himself than he should. Understandably! This place of strength must have felt quite heady and invigorating. Paul faced a temptation that many leaders do, namely, assuming that a dramatic experience of God's presence or a profound perception of God's voice is evidence of special worthiness on his part. I'm sometimes tempted to take credit for what is actually an undeserved gift. I take pride in my confident faith, leadership success, or the assumption that I'm making better spiritual progress than others around me. I may be tempted to believe that this favored experience of God is because of something special about *me* rather than evidence of God's kindness, goodness, and his reaching out to me.

So, as Paul puts it, God allows him to experience pain "to keep [him] from becoming conceited": Paul says he "was given a thorn in [his] flesh." It's hard for me to connect *given* and *thorn*. If I were to make a list of gifts I hope God will give me, a thorn would not be not on it. But, for Paul's own protection, God gave him a thorn.

What was this thorn in Paul's flesh? Some scholars suggest it was a tormenting physical condition. Others propose it was the continual conflict he experienced with the Christians at Corinth. Still others see the thorn as some form of unrelenting spiritual opposition. Perhaps it was some combination of these possibilities. It's helpful to us, however, that Paul isn't specific about the exact nature of this thorn. If he were, we might easily assume that his experience doesn't help us because we haven't experienced a similar thorn.

Whatever the thorn was, it was fueled by evil intention ("a messenger of Satan") and included very real torment. It was something in Paul's life that felt as if Satan were somehow having his way. This thorn was an unrelenting, painful reality in his life that must have felt like a place of great defeat.

No wonder this thorn becomes a place of great felt need in Paul's life. I know how that works. Over the years pain has had a way of focusing me, slowing me down. (I share a bit about this in my chapter "Suffering: Unexpected Unhurrying" in *An Unhurried Life*.) When I feel strong, I often feel little sense of need. Things are going my way—or at least the way I prefer. Perhaps much that I touch turns to gold. But then along comes a thorn and it digs at me. It annoys me. It torments me.

Nineteenth-century preacher Charles Spurgeon understood:

> Should you be favored with visions and revelations of the Lord, caught up to the third heaven, admitted into Paradise, and privileged to hear things which it was not lawful for a man to utter, conclude not that you have escaped the rod; rather expect that such high privilege will need heavy afflictions to balance it. If God has given you the great sail and the prosperous wind, he will also give you the heavy ballast to keep your keel deep in the stream.

It is far too easy to assume that exciting experiences of God are evidence of deeper life transformation or spiritual maturity than is actually true. Such moments may catalyze significant change, but change involves navigating challenges that cause me to rely on the Lord as I never have before and entering into disciplines that stretch me and test me. Profound encounters with God may carve a channel in me for the flow of God's life through me, but that flow will come (to mix my metaphors) as a fruit of my rootedness in the true vine.

These rich and life-changing moments with God create a practical challenge for us. When we pridefully take credit for good things that we experience or do that are actually evidence of God's generosity, we find ourselves in the unexpected place of being in opposition to our Lord. We don't mean for this to happen, but it does.

Paul's thoughts about the temptation to pride align with the practical counsel of James and Peter. James says that God "gives us more grace. That is why Scripture says: 'God opposes the proud but shows favor to the humble'" (Jas 4:6). Peter urges, "clothe yourselves with humility toward one another, because, 'God opposes the proud but shows favor to the humble'" (1 Pet 5:5). Success that comes as a result of human pride is not rooted in God's favor. In fact, human pride and God's grace are mutually exclusive. If I am not living in and empowered by God's grace, I am living in opposition to him.

As I've been thinking about pride and ministry, I've come to the humbling conclusion that pride has often been an engine for my apparent leadership success in the past, and I have seen this in too many other Christian leaders over the years. This truth really hit home when I took my training in spiritual direction at a Benedictine monastery in New Mexico. I lived in that community for a month at the beginning of my training and then for another two weeks at the end. Those bookends to my training highlighted for me the monks' graced humility that brought into stark relief the pride that has been, sadly, too common among leaders in my own Protestant evangelical tradition. Again, at times pride actually seems an engine that drives much church and nonprofit leadership activity. Too often Christian leaders I've bumped into—as well as the leader I've been myself—assume that they have the right answers to every question and that everyone else would do well to simply submit to their wisdom. There is a profound lack of humility regarding what we (think we) know or understand. Too rarely are leaders able to honestly say, "I can be wrong." Those four words are a beautiful (and true) statement of humility.

PERSISTENCE IN PRAYER

Paul's response to this tormenting thorn was to ask God to remove it. That's how I respond to thorns. I want hardships relieved or removed and weaknesses strengthened. Paul says that three times he "pleaded with the Lord to take [this thorn] away" (2 Cor 12:8). Paul undoubtedly prayed passionately and persistently for the resolution and relief that would have come with the removal of the thorn.

To be honest, many of my prayers are similar. When I feel physically ill or when someone I love is sick, I pray for healing. Is that wrong? Of course not. When I face relational conflicts with no finish line in sight, I ask for God's Spirit to bring reconciliation and restoration. When circumstances frustrate me or work against me, I pray for God's intervention. There is nothing wrong with that. God enjoys the communion of our childlike trust and dependence when we pray, "God! Heal me! Deliver me! Resolve it!"

Author and speaker Jill Briscoe shares her experience:

> In my desert of despondency I learned the life message that the basis of all spiritual strength is helplessness and dependence, and so God was not surprised at my desperate "I've had it, Lord" cry. On the contrary, He had been waiting around the corner of my self-effort to see me come to "wit's end corner" and throw myself on Him.

I have learned that it is far more fruitful and life giving to first seek God's person, his guiding presence, rather than resolution, healing, or situational improvement. And learning that lesson has usually involved a thorn.

AN UNANTICIPATED ANSWER: GRACE IS ENOUGH

The Lord answers Paul's request with "My grace is sufficient for you, for my power is made perfect in weakness" (2 Cor 12:9). Is this the answer Paul was seeking? Of course not! He wanted resolution, and

God did not give it. And instead of removing the thorn, the Lord explained to Paul that what he needed more than removal of the thorn was God's grace. God promised Paul that his empowering grace would be sufficient in this unresolved situation.

As I've already confessed, I had very different ideas about needing grace when I was a new Christian. In light of the big mess I felt I'd made in my life, I imagined that I was at the high point of my need for God's grace. I thought that over time I would need less and less grace until I hardly needed any at all because of course I would have my life mostly in order and be stumble and struggle free. Decades later, I've found the exact opposite to be true. The amount of grace I knew I needed in the first few years pales next to the greater need for grace that I am aware of now. I can't do anything with value in the kingdom apart from God and his grace.

My awareness of my need for God's grace enables me to seek and receive it. And that's a pattern I know well. I can't come to wholeness if I don't acknowledge my brokenness. I won't find healing if I don't acknowledge my wounds. And I can't grow in holiness until I tell the truth about my temptations and stumbling. Yet I didn't learn this important principle in my early years of leadership. Instead, what I saw modeled and therefore learned was that leaders are supposed to hide their weaknesses. It was clear to me that I was to put forth the image of a leader who had achieved a respectable level of godliness this side of heaven. So I spoke about temptation as though I were never actually tempted and about sin as though I were largely sin free. Projecting this image didn't help me because what I hid grew. Maintaining this image also didn't help those I led because they assumed that the struggles in their lives were unique to them and that they were doomed to a substandard experience of the Christian life. They may have been able to admire Pastor Alan, but follow his example of godliness? Never!

I learned that when I'm honest about my stumbling, people seem to find courage and hope for their own struggles. I'm not talking about making every teaching an exercise in discouraging self-revelation. I am talking about following the blessed counsel of Psalm 32: speaking the truth about my shortcomings and line crossings rather than hiding them, experiencing the freedom that comes from being forgiven by God, and living out that joyous freedom in the presence of those I lead. And you have only had a glimpse of my necessary growth in grace. Now, as I invite others to join me in that journey, I am not dispensing theoretical grace that I've read about. I can share with other people real grace that has touched my heart and empowered my life. When people are suffering, hopeless, tempted, hurting, or overwhelmed, they need real grace that we are able to give because we have actually received it. Real grace never gives easy answers to troubles, and comforting counsel is richly seasoned in real grace.

So God does not grant Paul's prayer for healing or resolution; instead the Lord awakens the apostle's mind and heart to his great and all-sufficient grace. And when God tells Paul that his grace will be sufficient, he isn't saying, "I know you wanted resolution, but you'll have to settle for grace." God knows we may discover that receiving grace is even better than resolution of the thorn we want removed. I wonder if this isn't what the psalmist means when he says that God's love is better than life (Ps 63:3).

But as a rule, living with unresolved hardship doesn't sound much like grace. This is a place for us to learn to humbly depend on God in a place of continually felt need. Jean-Pierre de Caussade, an eighteenth-century spiritual director and writer, suggested that "to make humility your foundation stone, the God of goodness begins by making you more keenly aware of your weakness. Yet when this feeling casts you down, at once let hope pick you up; for, as you know, it pleases God to turn our greatest weaknesses into triumphs for his grace." In a sense, Paul comes to understand that when God does not answer his prayers in the affirmative, the Lord might be offering a better response to a different question. God provides empowerment instead of relief, companionship instead of resolution. At first this may feel disappointing and puzzling, yet countless Christians through the centuries can testify to the wonders and richness of God's sustaining and sufficient grace.

GOD'S POWER, NOT MY PLANNING

One experience of the "grace is enough" dynamic came early in my ministry. My first church leadership experience was as a volunteer in the high school group, and one of the main objectives of our leadership team was to develop our communication skills. The youth pastor was a gifted and popular speaker at camps and conferences, so I was eager to learn everything I could from him. Unfortunately—I realized years later—I used what I learned to manipulate the students to whom I was speaking. I prided myself on knowing just where to put the emotionally charged story or the twist that would surprise the students. I knew how to appeal to their sense of guilt, inadequacy, and needing to do something for God. I was also seeking the students' admiration and affirmation to fill an aching hunger for recognition and a sense of value deep in my soul.

Later, when I was the pastor to a church's college ministry, I was still using those communication tricks to attract and keep the students' interest. It was at about this time, though, that I also became more seriously engaged in spiritual formation and more reliant on my communion with God as the engine for my life and ministry. God's very real power and my communication techniques began to feel at odds with one another.

Then came a time in my office that I will never forget. As was my habit, I was studying and preparing for an upcoming Sunday morning gathering. In the past, I had always been able to craft precise notes with well-placed illustrations, stories, and plot twists, but that day I found myself completely disabled. No matter how hard I tried, I could not produce the sort of message I was so accustomed to and, frankly, skilled at preparing and delivering. I had spent hours studying and praying over the passage I was planning to teach from, but the teaching notes would not come together.

On Sunday morning I found myself without a single note from which to speak to the students. As I waited for the worship songs to finish, I was feeling terrified. I envisioned this being the shortest teaching moment of my entire ministry. It would last, I figured, just about as long as it would take to read the passage I had chosen. *What would the students think? Was I never going to be able to teach effectively again?*

The inevitable moment came, and I stood before the students. I felt self-conscious and sweaty. I decided the only option I had was to open my Bible and read the passage. When I finished, I would tell the students that's all I had to say this morning—and I had no idea what would happen after that. As I was reading the passage aloud to the students, though, a meaningful thought or two surfaced in my mind and heart. I was sensing God's Spirit bringing this passage alive for me. I determined, even as I read, to at least share those thoughts after I'd finished reading, and that would be it. I wouldn't be lengthening the message much, and the morning would still be an utter failure.

As I started sharing ways that this passage had become for me a place of communion with God, I began to sense joy, inspiration, and empowerment. Those two personal insights became a rush of teaching that lasted at least as long as I usually spoke. But more important than the length was the message: it was so different from my former way. Before, my communication style was characterized by many references to myself, usually made in a self-promoting manner. This time my teaching was self-revealing, but in a way that seemed to draw attention to Jesus rather than to me. I was inviting these students to see in Scripture God's personal invitation to them to live in abiding relationship with him.

At the end of that message, as students had in the past, some came up to offer feedback. I usually heard comments like "Great message, Alan" or "You nailed me, Alan." This time, though, the comments were different. Students shared with me something personal about their own communion—or lack thereof—with Jesus. Rather than praising me, the students were focused on Jesus. And—by God's grace—instead of missing the post-teaching recognition fix, I found myself feeling a rich sense of peace and gratitude as I listened to them.

This pattern continued for a while. I would spend hours preparing to teach, but my efforts to create well-crafted message notes bore no fruit. Instead, I began to realize that my preparation had as much to do with preparing *myself* as it did with preparing a message. Oh, I wasn't standing up in front of the college group and winging it from week to week. During the week I was allowing Jesus to meet me deeply and personally, and then on Sundays I was sharing the overflow of that encounter. Sharing my personal journey seemed to speak more deeply to the students I served than my bag of communication tricks ever had.

Now, I share this story not as a recommended approach to effective teaching. I would never teach this method of preparation and communication to people new to church or ministry leadership. Yet my story may have prompted you to ask, do I really have to choose between excellent style and deep substance? I don't think so. These days, I again have quite a few thoughts written down and right in front of me when I speak to a group. I tell you this story, though, to share how God moved me from my attachment to certain communication tricks to sharing with those I taught God's living and personal truth. In me was an attachment to a structure that needed to die and, later, be resurrected. I think that's a pretty common pattern, and certainly a biblical one.

What I learned is that unhurried leadership functions most effectively when it is rooted in a place of lived-out resurrection.

THE PARADOX OF GRACE

Paul has come to see places of infirmity, verbal opposition, pressure and pain, harassment and aggravation as the very places where God's grace can rest on him, empower him, and give him peace and hope.

Paul has learned that God pours out his grace on places of human need. Paul is therefore able to say that he delights in experiences of weakness, insult, hardship, persecution, and difficulty because he's discovered that only in these places is he truly strong.

After saying that he delights in his weaknesses, Paul says to the proud and self-reliant church at Corinth, "When I am weak, then I am strong" (2 Cor 12:10). This line summarizes the main lesson learned from the thorn in his side. But other experiences—his dramatic encounter with God, the visions and revelations he saw, as well as these places of unresolved pain and prayers God answers in a completely unexpected way—also helped Paul learn how God's grace strengthens him as a man and as a leader.

David Bosch, a twentieth-century South African missiologist and theologian, connected this strength-in-weakness theme with leadership when he said,

> Being unknown, dying, disciplined, in sorrow and poverty are the true marks of an apostle. Weakness is an authentic characteristic of the apostolic ministry. Without the weakness which his opponents deride, there can be no real apostolic ministry and no true proclamation of Christ. The church is not made up of spiritual giants; only broken men can lead others to the cross. It is on men like Peter that Jesus builds His church. The possibility of change and conversion is based on humans being vulnerable; it does not, however, involve the vulnerability only of the one whom we would like to convert but also our own vulnerability as missionaries.

Returning to 2 Corinthians 12:10—"When I am weak, then I am strong"—note that *when* and *then* are concurrent, not consecutive. I find this significant because I have often wanted the grace of Christ's strength to come after my weakness is gone; I want his strength to replace my feeling of weakness. In other words, I assumed that when

I was weak, God would come along, take away weakness, and replace it with power. Logically, then, I also assumed that God would always remove the thorns from my life. Basically, I was seeing the grace of God as an enhancement to my strength rather than as strength in itself to be contained in the simple pottery of my weak little life. What we resist is the movement from apparent strength to apparent weakness. What Paul talks about is an acknowledgment of actual weakness, which becomes a place where the true strength of God's grace is perfected.

Paul is telling us that in the place of our felt weakness, we become more fully aware of the grace of Christ enabling, energizing, and guiding our thoughts, our words, our steps. Paul's experience illustrates that God's purposes are broader than our own, that he is interested not merely in the resolution of our hardships but in the extension of his kingdom truth and his very kingdom through those tough times.

PRACTICE: *PERSONALIZE SCRIPTURE*

For a few minutes, think about where you have been feeling weak. Have you been asking Christ to remove the weakness? What if he wants you to know his gracious strength in the midst of that weakness? What might that look like?

When I study 2 Corinthians 12, I find myself simply wanting to pray what I'm hearing Paul say. Try writing out your own prayer, following the themes of the text. Here's an example of how I started.

Some things about my life and ministry are noteworthy, but no one is going to gain much if I spend my time boasting about them. I am grateful for the wonderful things you have shown me and done in front of me through the years. (Honestly, Father, I don't know at all how to respond to you in the light of Paul's inexpressible experience in paradise. I guess I shouldn't feel too bad when he didn't know how to put it into words either!) So, if any boasting is to be done, it needs to be boasting by which I decrease and you increase. Speaking the truth about myself is good, but I'm not aiming at improving others' opinion of me. Use me to improve their opinion of you.

Unhurried Leadership Reflections

1. What is our culture's attitude toward weaknesses? How do people deal with their own weaknesses? How do they respond to the weaknesses of others?

2. What are some of the ways you have witnessed God at work in and through your weaknesses? In what ways have you discovered that a lack of resolution did not mean a lack of God's favor? (Your experiences don't have to be as dramatic as Paul's to be meaningful and important.)

3. What experiences do you have with unresolved difficulties in your life or ministry at this point in your spiritual journey? Using your God-guided imagination, can you envision ways that these could be opportunities for grace to be on display in and through you?

4. As you reflect on Paul's insight into strength graciously perfected in our weakness, how might this affect the way you pray? Where have you been tempted to hide your weaknesses—even in prayer? How might you open up and pour out your heart to God about these weaknesses?

5. God decided not to remove the thorn from Paul's life, but instead gave Paul sufficient grace. How might you see your own difficulties as Paul did—as ways for the power of Christ to be with you more constantly? Ask God's Spirit for insight.

EIGHT

Unhurrying Our Thoughts

RECENTLY, THE PRACTICE OF NOTICING my thoughts has become a transforming and empowering activity for me. I've come to realize how many thoughts have been in my thinking for so long that their slight whisper can trigger in me a far-from-slight reaction.

What does she really think of me?

How will I ever get this project done?

Why is he taking so long?

These thoughts have, in fact, become habits. As such, they have grabbed me and sometimes pressed me into unhelpful and unholy responses. I call them "autopilot thoughts" because too often they seem to be thinking me more than I am thinking them.

You've probably heard it said that "you are what you eat." In physical terms, every cell in our bodies has been built out of and nourished by the things we have eaten over recent weeks as well as past months and even years. If we have cultivated good eating habits, our bodies have benefitted. When it comes to our inner life, an echo of this insight is the idea that "we are what we think." The thoughts that we allow to make themselves at home in our minds and hearts shape our souls. Some of those thoughts are good, true, and life-giving; some of them are not. Some of the thoughts that run through my mind feel like my own, some feel like gifts from God, and some feel like the whispers of an enemy.

Martin Laird, who has written some helpful things on the Christian practice of contemplation, suggests this: "If we think we are our thoughts and feelings, we go through life simply reacting to what is going on around us, with little awareness that we are even doing this or that life could be otherwise. When we try to pray, distractions will strike us as being especially ensnaring, even overwhelming." So as I engage in noticing my thoughts, it helps me to remember that the thoughts that run through my mind are not necessarily *me*. I *have* thoughts. For example, temptations come as thoughts. At times the voice of the enemy whispers leading suggestions from the back of my mind that seem to be my own thoughts. Messages from the world seep in via television and social media. If I mindlessly embrace these thoughts as my own, they may too often prompt my next action taken or word spoken.

When I pay attention to my thoughts, I also realize how many different thoughts run through my mind. I have thoughts about my life, my wife and my sons, my friends, my work, food, and play. Some of these thoughts are rooted in truth and end up bearing good fruit in my life and my work, but some don't take me to good places. Some thoughts are God-given and Spirit-inspired, while others are downright diabolical. Some thoughts seem my own, though they may echo either the voice of a loving heavenly Father or the whispers of my soul's enemy. And some thoughts are just plain mundane.

INVITE GOD'S LOVING GAZE

David's prayer in Psalm 139 has proven especially helpful to me in this matter of dealing with my thoughts.

Search me, God, and know my heart;
    test me and know my anxious thoughts.
See if there is any offensive way in me,
    and lead me in the way everlasting. (vv. 23-24)

Here David welcomes God's loving, all-knowing gaze into the depths of his heart. Following David's example, we can pour out our hearts to our heavenly Father. In fact, the Spirit can shed light on thoughts that have become embedded as impulses and enable us to shut or at least slow them down. But letting God search my heart requires me to slow down enough to be searched. If I'm going through airport security, I have to submit myself to being searched. I can't run through the line and avoid X-ray machines or TSA agents. Similarly, a kind of inward stopping is required if God is to search our hearts. Practically speaking, I can sit down in a comfortable chair and become physically still in a relatively short time. But it takes longer for my mind and heart to become still in God's presence so that he might search my soul.

David prays, "Search me, God, and know my heart." Too often, instead of inviting the searching eyes of God to know my heart, I hide what is in my heart from myself, from others, and—as if it's even possible—from God. I'm not that different from our first father and mother, who tried hiding in the garden when God called for them. I'm like a little child who imagines that, since he has his hands over his eyes and can't see anything, no one can see him either. We play along with such a child, and perhaps God lovingly condescends to our silly little game, but eventually the path of a life worth living is found in being deeply known by our God.

David's prayer continues: "Test me and know my anxious thoughts." Similarly, I invite God to "test" what he has searched out in me, especially my anxious thoughts—and I define *anxious thoughts* as every thought that is not rooted in my trust in God. I have realized that so many of my thoughts seem to take absolutely no notice of the real presence of God with me—caring for me, protecting me, guiding me, affirming me, encouraging me. I too often lack confidence in God's measureless faithfulness. I sometimes allow troubles to loom larger than the ever-present and almighty God who has good plans for my life. I'm tempted to hide rather than submit my heart and mind to the gaze of the God who loves me, the One who wishes only to heal, free, guide, and empower me to walk more closely with him.

The next line of David's prayer also needs to be mine: "See if there is any offensive way in me." These offensive ways are more than my mere anxiety. God can see in me certain traits that actually are offensive to him. Think of an offensive smell. You step in something, and the smell travels with you. Just as we do what we can to avoid such smells, I'm tempted to do what I can to hide from God anything in me that he would find offensive. I want to put on my best appearance. But let's remember that the God we invite to search us is *for* us, not against us. God is against what may damage or destroy us or others, but even then God is for us. When God searches us, we shouldn't be surprised that anxious or offensive thoughts surface. He reveals them in order to quiet them, cleanse us, and renew our minds. Any anxious or toxic thought in me is perfectly safe to bring into the presence of the God who seeks my good.

The last line of David's prayer brings hope and encouragement: "Lead me in the way everlasting." Having invited God to see me as I am, I can then be led in the way of life he has for me. I find, however, that as I walk in God's way, he brings to light those thoughts that shouldn't be in my mind and heart. Yielding myself to this is easier when I, like David, remember what I know about this God who is searching my heart:

> How precious to me are your thoughts, God!
>   How vast is the sum of them!
> Were I to count them,
>   they would outnumber the grains of sand—
>   when I awake, I am still with you. (Ps 139:17-18)

David acknowledges here just how "precious" God's vast and priceless thoughts are, quite a contrast to his own anxious and sometimes offensive thoughts. David longed to be led in the way of lasting life by the One who is always thinking the good, the beautiful, and the true toward him. Sharing in that longing, I bring my anxious thoughts into the presence of God's peace. I bring my fearful thoughts into the presence of his encompassing love. I bring my discouragement into the presence of eternal encouragement. I bring my self-doubt into the presence of the faithful one.

HELP FROM THE DESERT

One source of help in this matter of noticing our thoughts is the tradition of the desert fathers and mothers of the early centuries of the church. These men and women left behind their cities and journeyed into the deserts of Egypt, Israel, and other wilderness regions of the Middle East. They went, in part, to escape what they saw as the easy faith of an official church and, in part, to follow in the footsteps of Jesus, who was led by the Spirit into the wilderness (Lk 4:1-2). In seeking to escape the corruption they saw in their urban worlds, they soon discovered that the wilderness held as many temptations to sin as the cities. In other words, they realized the battle was as much within them as it was surrounding them.

Among the legacy of these early Christians is the identification of what came to be known as the seven deadly sins, although they're more like eight deadly thoughts. The categories identified were thoughts about food, sex, things, anger, dejection, acedia, vainglory, and pride. (The later listing of seven deadly sins combined the similar vices of vainglory and pride.) The desert fathers and mothers learned that a life of godliness begins with the practice of noticing our thoughts, especially those that are anxious or even offensive.

When people went out to the desert to learn from these holy men and women, they were encouraged to honestly and openly share whatever thoughts went through their minds. Rather than waiting for negative thoughts to become negative perspectives, behaviors, or, worse, habits, these believers addressed where all such things begin: in our thoughts. They mentored new members of their communities in how to become more awake to their thoughts. Before they settled in as unquestioned assumptions, shaped expectations, or captured wills, these bad thoughts were noticed and addressed.

COUNTLESS THOUGHTS TO NOTICE

When I first began intentionally paying attention to my thoughts, I found myself thinking about a scene from an *I Love Lucy* episode. Lucy and Ethel are working on a candy factory assembly line, and they are supposed to wrap the individual chocolates that are coming by on a conveyer belt so they can be boxed up further down the line. At first, the chocolates come along at a moderate pace, and Lucy and Ethel keep up just fine. Eventually, though, the conveyer belt begins to accelerate until the two friends are no longer keeping up. What to do with all the chocolates? Thinking quickly and quite resourcefully, the women begin to stuff chocolate into their mouths and down their shirts. Too many chocolates coming at them way too fast! Just like my thoughts come at me. So many of them are coming so quickly, and too often I feel that I'm at their mercy. Even that is a thought. With all these thoughts, I feel like I can't afford to pay attention to each one unless my full-time job is "thought noticer," and no one's paying me to do that job.

Are you, like me, always thinking? Then you may also imagine getting lost in your thoughts, and in thoughts about your thoughts, and so on. I usually find that noticing a few of my thoughts slows my thinking down. I experience a holy unhurry in the practice. If I miss a thought and it's important, the Lord will bring it back around at some point. The practice of noticing our thoughts begins by ... simply noticing our thoughts—strategic or mundane, inspiring or anxious, interesting or boring.

When I pay attention to the immediate thought before me, it no longer seems part of the swarm. One by one, my thoughts feel less overwhelming. Theologian and professor Martin Laird suggests that "the key is to move from being a victim of thoughts (the commenting, chattering mind) to being their witness (the heart's stillness). Thoughts and feelings remain, but this move from victim to witness transforms our relationship with affliction." The role of witness enables me to look at my thoughts as separate from me, which, after all, they are.

One practice that helps me notice my thoughts is journaling. It's often a helpful way for me to sample the stream of thoughts running through my mind at any given moment. Just now, for example, I took five minutes to write down whatever thoughts went through my mind. I tried to capture in words both the content and the feeling of each thought. In five minutes I wrote down nearly twenty thoughts. Ten percent of them were positive and ninety percent were negative or mundane. (Can you see why I need this practice?) Some thoughts feel meaningful; some feel boring. Some feel restful and some anxious. At this point I don't take much time to assess them. I notice them. I see them. Again, I try to become conscious of streams of thought that too often flow through my mind unnoticed.

Another simple way to notice my thoughts is to set aside a few minutes to just be still and silent. Although I am quiet on the outside, my mind is rarely quiet within. Thoughts bubble into consciousness. As they do, I try to notice them. I resist the temptation to let one of them provoke me to give up on the quiet and get busy doing something. (There are plenty of good things to be done on any given day. In this moment, though, I am intentionally paying attention to the thoughts that enter my awareness when I'm quiet.) If I sit long enough, a few thoughts will inevitably come back, persistently knocking on the door of my mind again, like a door-to-door salesperson who hasn't yet met his quota.

Just bringing these thoughts out from the shadows of my subconscious into the light of my awareness can be incredibly freeing. We begin by simply noticing the thoughts, no matter how boring, significant, fearsome, or inviting they may seem. We are wise to seek to be awake and attentive to the thoughts that cross our minds. At first, we are only trying to notice our thoughts and gain a little bit of distance from them and perspective on them. Many thoughts seem to arise on their own. Thoughts that cross our minds may actually be the gift of a loving Father or echoes of our truest self. Some may indeed be traps of the enemy or whispers from our old self. When I am not noticing my thoughts, they end up directing my life in ways I may not appreciate.

In addition to the endless internal stream of ideas, we are bombarded by so many messages from our information-saturated world that we can easily become overwhelmed. Decades ago, professor and spiritual writer Douglas Steere suggested that "the hail of irrelevant stimuli to which our modern life seems increasingly to subject us . . . [and] the pressure and temporarily satisfying narcotic of intense busyness in outward occupations—these all seem to make us bent on distracting rather than on gathering ourselves." If we are not making an effort to notice our thoughts, we are likely either letting ourselves be distracted by them or using them to keep ourselves distracted. In a world that assaults our hearts and minds with an endless stream of messages, it is indeed a challenge to discern our thoughts.

Wanting to give our attention to our thoughts is the first step on this challenging path. We all, for instance, know about those thoughts that jump around when we seek to be still and pay attention to what's happening in our hearts and minds. Henri Nouwen put it this way:

> As soon as I decide to stay in my solitude, confusing ideas, disturbing images, wild fantasies, and weird associations jump about in my mind like monkeys in a banana tree. Anger and greed begin to show their ugly faces. I give long, hostile speeches to my enemies and dream lustful dreams in which I am wealthy, influential, and very attractive—or poor, ugly, and in need of immediate consolation.

This image has helped me in at least two ways. First, I don't jump up into the tree to argue with the monkeys and demand they stop their chatter. This only stirs them up more. Second, if I'm patient, the monkeys finally get tired and quiet their chatter. I need to be calm and patient when I settle myself in an effort to recognize what is happening in my heart and mind.

As we prayerfully seek to notice our thoughts, we may find that "our bodies may be at the place of prayer, but our minds are usually not where our bodies are, but instead are at a shopping mall; on a beach; . . . reliving an argument; fearing the future; regretting the past; any place but right here in the simplicity of the present moment." Noticing our thoughts requires that we let our minds slow down until they are present with us in the moment. Being spiritually, mentally, and emotionally present where we are is another important aspect of this challenging work.

DISCERNING OUR THOUGHTS

Once I've noticed the thoughts running through my mind, it helps to determine where they are coming from. For example, at some point of my life, I started thinking of my more negative, self-centered, and sour thoughts as childish or juvenile. I had plenty of good days in my childhood and youth, but I had some bad ones as well. We all do. In addition, I did not always live in a way that reflected the reality of God's kingdom, goodness, or life-giving way for me. This behavior resulted in patterns of thought that became habitual, and eventually began directing much of my life without my even being aware of their existence, much less their power.

In addition to paying attention to thoughts, I find it helpful to notice the emotions that accompany them. Thoughts accompanied by anxiety, panic, insecurity, discouragement, or despair, for example, aren't flowing from the presence of God. On the other hand, thoughts that are accompanied by deep peace, buoyant joy, solid hope or selfless sympathy for others are more likely to be flowing from God's presence. The emotions that attend our thoughts are a helpful clue as to their source.

Also worth noticing is whether our thoughts are passing ideas or firmly held convictions, well-ensconced assumptions, and long-standing expectations. We are wise to note whether our thoughts are life giving or destructive, shortsighted or transcendent, unsettling or soothing, self-serving or God-honoring. But again, what I need to start with is simply noticing the thoughts I think—doing so in the presence of the One who made me able to think. Author and spiritual director Mary Margaret Funk shares this observation: "Thoughts that are thought about become desires. Desires that are thought about become passions. Good thoughts become virtues. Bad thoughts become bad desires; bad passions or habits of action become sins. The passions are acted upon us when we consent, then the passions move from passive to active engagement." Taking initiative to notice and discern our thoughts is wisely proactive, empowering, and freeing.

When we intentionally and prayerfully notice our thoughts, we are not emptying our minds, but focusing them. Speaking on God's behalf, Paul charged us to do exactly that: "Since, then, you have been raised with Christ, set your hearts on things above, where Christ is, seated at the right hand of God. Set your minds on things above, not on earthly things" (Col 3:1-2). Setting our minds and hearts on Christ brings stability and rootedness. Still, some believers fear that silent prayer or contemplation is equivalent to a dangerous emptying of our minds, perhaps in the spirit of Jesus' parable about the person out of whom a demon is cast, leaving the house of his soul unoccupied and in danger of an even worse infestation (Mt 12:43-45). But our quiet prayer is actually our living more fully with Jesus residing in the home of our heart rather than being absent from it.

SAY NO WITH SCRIPTURE

In his response to Satan's temptations in the wilderness, Jesus offers us a great example to follow (Lk 4). To each of the three temptations, Jesus responds with a simple line of Scripture.

Evagrius of Pontus, a desert father from the fourth century, applied Jesus' approach to temptations to the eight deadly thoughts and developed a sort of manual for spiritual battle titled *Talking Back: A Monastic Handbook for Combating Demons*. Since you are probably not a monk, you might not identify precisely with his approach to the Scriptures or the specific temptations he mentions, but his wisdom is undeniable. We can learn to resist those negative thoughts that arise in our minds and hearts with a simple word of scriptural truth. Evagrius realized that our thoughts make a great difference in how we live and therefore need to be taken seriously. He trained himself and his students to notice thoughts, discern their content, and then respond or resist as appropriate.

Some of my negative thoughts are actually attacks leveled against me by the enemy of my soul. If I remain passive, they can overwhelm me, but I can choose resistance in place of passivity. Our opposition to the attacks needs to be active, but the opposition isn't difficult. With just a line of scriptural truth, we can respond to the suggestions of the tempter. Letting thoughts from the enemy sit corrosively in our thinking and feelings allows them to eat away at our confidence, peace, joy, courage, energy.

In addition to wielding Scripture against the enemy, we can heed Paul's charge in 2 Corinthians 10:3-5:

> Though we live in the world, we do not wage war as the world does. The weapons we fight with are not the weapons of the world. On the contrary, they have divine power to demolish strongholds. We demolish arguments and every pretension that sets itself up against the knowledge of God, and we take captive every thought to make it obedient to Christ.

Here Paul describes the nature of the battle in which the followers of Christ find themselves. This battle is not primarily an outward one, but an internal one. Instead of destroying buildings or making prisoners of enemy combatants, we "demolish arguments and every pretension . . . and we take captive every thought." These arguments are our enemies and enemies to the cause of Christ because they are set up against knowledge of God and submission to Jesus' reign. Such thoughts find their way into the shadows of our minds and launch their quiet attacks from those hidden places. Thankfully, God has given us divine weapons that can demolish arguments contradicting who God truly is and what he does. We resist those thoughts that do not resonate with his kingdom reality. In this passage Paul speaks of some thoughts as "strongholds." These strongly held yet often hidden assumptions, expectations, attitudes, views, or arguments are in direct and complete opposition to Jesus and his kingdom. That they linger beneath the surface of our awareness adds to the strength of their hold on us: we can't battle what we don't see. When a sense of hopelessness joins the oppression of the enemy's lies, these strongholds become even stronger.

BREAKING A NEGATIVE THOUGHT-HABIT

Anyone who has known me for very long knows that I have had a cyclical issue with my weight. I've lost weight. I've gained weight. I've rinsed and repeated this cycle more times than I can count. As I've been writing this chapter, I have sensed again God's Spirit nudging me in this area of my thinking. In many ways this cycle is an issue rooted in my thoughts about food.

On one occasion, as I was thinking about my plan to return to a level of eating that would enable me to start losing a couple of pounds a week, the words of Jesus, quoting Deuteronomy, came to mind: "It is written: 'Man shall not live on bread alone, but on every word that comes from the mouth of God'" (Mt 4:4). The life in the

Scriptures is God's own life. It is life by which we are nourished *in relationship with the Lord.* The Word comes from the mouth of God and these words are being spoken even today. They are alive in the present, not just in the past.

Now, widening the angle of the lens, I hear Jesus, who has been fasting for forty days, say that his greatest need is not for bread (physical food) but for communication with the Father (spiritual food). My struggle with my weight has, in many ways, been a struggle with this very truth. In some part of me, I believe that I actually *do* live on bread—that which enters my mouth, goes down into my stomach, and exits the other end. But physical food does not nourish my inner life. My soul is not strengthened by my favorite potato chips or a beer or a steak or whatever it is—or however much of it—I eat.

The real Alan (as opposed to his body) lives on whatever it is that God says to me. God's words of truth and life are what will nourish me. Too often I have short-circuited this communication by seeking to find soul nourishment in the filling of my stomach. I have not taken Jesus' words or example to heart. I have believed what is untrue, and my body pays the consequences of this misguided attempt to find life in what I eat. The reason I want to learn to eat better is that my body does need good, healthy food, but only so much of it.

If I can join Jesus in eating less than I use for a season, I actually think this would honor God with my body. A healthy, more useable body would be a greater acknowledgment of God's ownership of it. I acknowledge the truth of this word. I want God to show me how to trust what he says here. It is true that I cannot satisfy my soul with fine food, but my soul can be satisfied *as though* I had enjoyed the finest meal money could buy (Ps 63:5).

Another practical example of this practice and its value comes in my work. Recently, I had a conversation with a friend in a similar ministry as mine. We were developing some places of mutual accountability in our work. One element of that mutual commitment was the certain number of phone calls I intended to make weekly in order to develop donors and invite leaders to the training we provide. Whenever I call someone I haven't met or don't know very well, I find these thoughts slithering around in the back of my mind: *My call is an imposition on this person's time. I am bothering them. They probably won't find what I have to say interesting.* Seeing them spelled out makes these thoughts sound a lot more juvenile than adult. It sounds like a teenage me who sometimes felt unimportant, unnoticed by others.

The mere act of bringing that thought into awareness provokes a number of responses to the expressed concern: *This person might very well be busy. Right now may not be a good time to talk, but perhaps we could plan another time to speak,* or *This person might actually be interested in the invitation I want to extend or the shared work I want to propose. Why would I deny them at least the opportunity to make that choice themselves?*

In addition to this practice of noticing and discerning my thoughts, I've found it helpful to take initiative with my thoughts. We hear, for instance, the psalmist talking to himself when he says, "Why, my soul, are you downcast?" (Ps 42:5). Here is a way in which I can be observing my thoughts. Jeremiah did this in his Lamentations:

> I say to myself, "The LORD is my portion;
>   therefore I will wait for him."
>
> The LORD is good to those whose hope is in him,
>   to the one who seeks him;
> it is good to wait quietly
>   for the salvation of the LORD. (3:24-26)

In a place where there seems little hope of being filled, Jeremiah determined to wait in hope for God's goodness and salvation. This passage of Scripture gives me an opportunity to follow his example and remind myself of eternal kingdom reality as I face painful present realities.

PRACTICE: *UNHURRYING OUR THOUGHTS*

Table 1

Noticing	Discerning	Responding

I mentioned journaling as a tool that helps me both unhurry and discern my thoughts. Let me share a simple three-level framework that has been freeing and life giving for me. Begin by creating three columns, as in table 1.

First, I *notice* my stream-of-consciousness thoughts for five minutes. After setting the timer on my phone, I simply record the thoughts that bubble up into my heart and mind over those minutes. As I write them down, I try to note the emotional content these ideas bring with them. Sometimes the thoughts feel mundane ("I'm kind of hungry"); sometimes they seem pregnant with anxiety, joy, or hope. In this first step, I simply record them as accurately as I can.

Sometimes I'll feel as if I've reached the end of whatever thoughts I'm having. I'll think, *I'm not having any more thoughts.* It turns out that this is a thought, so I write it down. Or I might think, *That was a weird thought to have,* and I write down this opinion as one of my thoughts. At the end of five minutes, I stop writing.

The second step is to look back over the thoughts I've written down and ask myself, *What do I discern about this stream of thoughts?* Questions like the following help me identify where these thoughts are coming from and whether they are helpful or hurtful, life giving or life draining:

- Is this just a passing, rather mundane thought, or does it deserve more of my attention?

- Does this thought sound like me? Does it sound more like a friend or an enemy?

- If I spoke this thought out loud to myself, would it sound true or false? Affirming or degrading?

- If I spoke this thought to someone else, would it be heard as a word of grace or criticism, acceptance or judgment?

- Does this thought bring with it feelings of peace or anxiety, gratitude or complaint, hopefulness or despair, belonging or loneliness, and so on?

- Is the tone of my thoughts generally positive or negative?

Again, these questions can help me both unpack information about the source and identify the nature of the thoughts running through my head. When I've led a group through this exercise, they have found becoming aware of even just five minutes of thoughts very instructive.

The third and final element of this exercise is to determine how you will respond to the thoughts and insights. What action(s), if any, would you like to take, either in line with your thoughts or in resistance to them? Do I embrace this thought or stand against it—and what actions does that answer encourage? For example, I've discovered a few negative thoughts that surface just about every time I do this exercise. They are thoughts of anxiety or fear, self-doubt or insecurity. I've done this exercise enough to know that such thoughts are internal enemies that many of us are far too familiar with. These thoughts have sometimes felt so strong that I imagined them like the ringwraiths riding their black demon horses in *The Lord of the Rings*. But when I consider these thoughts in the context of God's presence, they begin to look a little more like hobbits riding Shetland ponies. That latter image emboldens me to resist whatever negative, deceptive, destructive aspects of my thoughts I've noticed. Then I address these thoughts specifically with a Scripture truth as Jesus did in the wilderness.

Noticing, discerning, responding—these three steps help me in a number of practical ways. Fairly regularly, for instance, they serve as a kind of mental hygiene at the beginning of my workday. At other times, if I feel inwardly stuck in the middle of my day, this three-part tool often helps me uncover the negative thinking behind that feeling. I also use this tool when I'm feeling overwhelmed by thoughts that seem in conflict with one another. Finally, walking through the noticing, discerning, responding steps has proven a useful problem-solving and decision-making tool for me.

This talk about becoming aware of our thoughts will seem daunting to some. Leaders who have great strengths as thinkers will probably not be as threatened as those who find their strengths in the doing. It is not one or the other though. Thinkers need to find their way to fruitful action; doers need to learn to reflect on the thoughts that lead to the actions they take. And this noticing, discerning, responding process helps both kinds of leaders.

One more point. If this practice of noticing your thoughts is new to you, this exercise will almost certainly feel a little clunky at first. Be patient. With practice, you may even find that you're able to notice your thoughts with a bit more perspective in the course of your day and not only when you intentionally engage the process.

Unhurried Leadership Reflections

1. What insights came from your experience with the three-step thought exercise? How do you notice God's presence in the midst of your thoughts? What thoughts feel more attacking than affirming?

2. Identify a specific negative thought in your life that feels like a long-standing bad habit. Is it anxiety? fear? self-doubt? lust? anger? What truth from Scripture might be a useful, simple, powerful weapon to use against such thoughts when you notice them?

3. With which trusted friend could you have a conversation of noticing thoughts? In the context of mutual confidentiality, share with one another some of the thoughts, positive or negative, that

bubble up in the moment. Acknowledge that these thoughts may be your own, or that they may come from another source. What do you notice together? What will you do to encourage one another in the effort to set your mind and heart on things above (Col 3:1-2)?

NINE

Prayer as Primary Influence

EARLY IN MY WORK AS A PASTOR, I often found maintaining a regular consistent prayer life a real challenge. I've since realized that one reason was I didn't see the connection between praying and leading. Praying seemed a mostly personal discipline of my faith. In my role as a leader, I tried to be faithful to opening leadership meetings in prayer and to praying before I did something for Jesus. That brief moment I spent praying at the beginning or before any kingdom work betrayed how little I valued the role of prayer in my leadership. At best, I saw prayer as preparatory to kingdom leadership rather than as an organic and essential engine for such leadership.

I'm not the only one who has misunderstood the role of prayer in ministry. I've spoken to friends working in a church or ministry that made it clear that prayer was something to be done on one's own time, probably in the morning before leaving for the office. No one had ever said to them, "We're not paying you to pray. We're paying you to manage programs and to make things happen." Obviously that would sound wrong to most ears, but that message seemed all too clearly implied. And what a contrast to leaders of the first-century church. Luke wrote that as the practical needs of people were multiplying and requiring more and more time and attention, the church leaders saw to it that mature and wise members of the community were attentive to those needs so they—as leaders—could continue to give their attention to "prayer and the ministry of the word" (Acts 6:4).

In my early days of ministry, I would have focused only on the "word" side of that statement and understood it primarily in terms of studying the Scriptures for the purpose of teaching or preaching. That is certainly appropriate, as far as it goes, but I now understand "the ministry of the word" to mean that key leaders in the Christian community must be men and women who listen well to God in interactive communion with him. Pastors and other Christian leaders need to have a sense of where God is leading and what God is saying to his people in a particular place and at a particular time. This sense—crucial to effective ministry as we guide real people to live simultaneously in this world and the reality of God's kingdom—is acquired through the ministry of the word and prayer. This kind of prayer is the sort of thing I imagine Epaphras doing when I read that he was "tireless in his prayers for [the Colossian Christians], praying that you'll stand firm, mature and confident in everything God wants you to do" (Col 4:12 *The Message*). Prayer isn't an activity apart from the work of ministry; prayer is a primary element of the actual work of ministry. And the only thing that can really get in the way of my engaging in this ministry is . . . me.

Leadership prayer is vital to being a person of godly influence, so it is always best as a first response rather than a last resort. After all, for any number of reasons (sin, logistics, priorities, commitments, and so on), I can't always speak or act in ways I want to, but I can always pray—anytime and anywhere. This sort of prayer for the good of others is a beautiful way to live out Jesus' great commandment to "love one another." This kind of prayer also awakens me to how significantly my praying for others affects how I relate to them and, in whatever way God has given me, how I might influence them for kingdom good.

LEARNING TO WORK WITH GOD

As a leader, I want to learn to follow the example of the Good Shepherd who "lives to intercede" for his people (Heb 7:25). As I abide in Jesus, I have the same access to the Father's ear that he does. I am able to interact with the Father in prayer and seek the good of those I care about, knowing that my prayer mysteriously opens a door to a greater experience of God's measureless love.

I think of Jesus' pattern of withdrawing from the crowd and even from his disciples to pray. I suspect in those times of prayer Jesus was remembering not only the Father's love for him expressed at his baptism but also the Father's love for the Twelve, the other followers, and the crowds who surrounded him day by day. Jesus withdrew from the crowds for the sake of the crowds. When Jesus was in prayer, he remembered that the Father's words matter far more than the words of the crowd, whether they were shouting "Hosanna!" or "Crucify him!" It was as though the Father said to Jesus as he prayed, "When you are in the wilderness, you are my beloved Son. When the crowds cheer for you and praise you, you are my beloved Son. When the crowds turn on you and cry out for your execution, you are my beloved Son."

I want to be a leader who follows this pattern of prayer we see in Jesus' life. When it comes to the rhythm of contemplation and action in the life of a leader, I think more of us have tended to neglect contemplation in favor of action rather than the reverse. We live in such an outward-focused leadership world. That's why I have sought to integrate contemplation and leadership over the last twenty-five years. Prayer really is *someone we are with* more than *something we do*. Prayer—being with Jesus—is a leader's greatest source of influence. Therefore, prayer must never be a merely peripheral activity for leaders.

Consider the wisdom of spiritual writer and director Baron Friedrich von Hügel in his declaration that the focus of ministry is really on helping souls:

> I wonder if you have seen how much you will be called on to help people—to help souls. The golden rule is, to help those we love to escape from us; and never try to begin to help people, or influence them, till they ask, but wait for them. Souls are never dittos. The souls thus to be helped are mostly at quite different stages from our own, or they have quite a different attrait. One should wait silent for those who do not open out to us, who are not intended, perhaps, ever to be helped by us—except by our prayers (the best of all helps). We must be tolerant and patient, too, with those we can, and ought to help. This difference in souls wakes us up, and makes us more sensitive and perceptive.

I like the gentleness of the approach to helping others that von Hügel describes. There can be violence when we assume that we know what another person needs. This is where learning to listen to God on behalf of others can help us learn to cooperate with what God may already be doing in their lives. Making prayer for others a primary activity in our spiritual leadership enables us to be a more effective partner with the Spirit regarding the work of God in the lives of his people. God is the master of souls, not me. But I can learn how to work with God to serve, bless, and care for those entrusted to my care.

Jean-Jacques Olier, a seventeenth-century French priest and spiritual director, spoke simply and powerfully about the role of prayer in ministry:

> Without personal prayer, our ministry will be empty, our words meaningless, our [ministry] totally fruitless. Without prayer we shall never be able to support souls in their weaknesses. They have given themselves to us as those upon whom they may trust, but without prayer we would be the cause of their falls, since they will

not find in us the strength and light they need. We being dark and weak ourselves, it is only by the means of prayer that we can be enlightened and made strong in Christ Jesus. All the failures which arise in the direction of souls come from the fact that directors do not apply themselves to the holy exercise of prayer.

It would help immensely if we saw our influence—our leadership—as the care of souls. Our most lasting influence in the lives of others is to enable them to become whole and holy in all the ways Jesus invites them. We can't do that without prayer. There are no shortcuts or surefire techniques apart from our vital and life-giving communion with God in prayer. This is the influence that will still matter to us centuries and millennia from now.

WHAT GOOD IS PRAYER?

"In prayer we discover what we already have," noted Thomas Merton, Trappist monk and author, toward the end of his life. He continued: "You start from where you are and you deepen what you already have, and you realize you are already there. We already have everything but we don't know it and don't experience it. Everything has been given to us in Christ. All we need is to experience what we already possess." Merton's point has much to say about our leadership prayer. In the ongoing work we do in our conversational relationship with God, we find out that we already have all we need to do every good thing God has given us to do in our lives, our relationships, and our work. We live in a kingdom where, if we seek it first, everything else necessary and good comes to us.

So, practically speaking, I find that when prayer for others is consistent and well established, I experience holy energy rising up from within me to do good work. Extended seasons of praying for people I serve in some role or leadership relationship ends up being very motivating. My compassion for people as well as my wisdom about how to help seem to increase. There also seem to be more divine surprises in my interactions with others when I've invested significant time holding them prayerfully in God's presence.

I've also noticed a fruitful connection between focusing my prayer on particular people and then finding in myself greater interest, curiosity, compassion, and engagement with those people. When my day-to-day prayer for particular people grows thin, however, I also find that my heart's inclination toward them and my interest in them diminish. Bringing people into God's presence through intercessory prayer keeps alive and vital their place in my heart. When prayer is thin, love is thin.

This practice raises my kingdom energy and engagement level. I have more kingdom interest in others rather than seeing them in relation to my own kingdom. I find it easier to engage in my roles and relationships of influence with the confident posture of a servant rather than from a needy and authoritarian posture. I find that when I am not praying much for others, not much flows through me toward them for their good—not much holy concern, not much spiritual interest, not much joyful attention. But when I am praying often and well for others, I find that I actually experience rivers of living water flowing from those who trust in him, just as Jesus promised (Jn 7:38).

PRAYER MAKES A DIFFERENCE

Another measurable fruit of praying for people is a practical one. Early in my ministry, I remember how often I would complain that I was just not good at remembering names, as though it were some unavoidable disability over which I was powerless. I knew of other pastors who seemed to have a limitless capacity for learning and recalling even the names of those who visited a service only once. As I began to embark on a way of ministry that was more oriented to the formation of people, I also began to pray in a more focused and intentional way for the people in my life—not just my family and close friends, but people who crossed my path in church gatherings or other social settings. I'm sure it won't surprise you that I began to remember their names more easily. When I took time to remember prayerfully in God's presence those who had been guests at a service, I found that a place opened up for them in my heart *and* in my memory. I remember what matters to me, and what matters to me—my treasure— is where my heart is, where my time is spent, where my attention tends to focus. I find a growing desire to invest my heart, time, and attention toward those whom God has called me to lead.

Also not surprising is that, rather than drawing energy away from and weakening my effectiveness, leadership rooted in prayer increases it. Put differently, as a Christian leader, I do not need to choose between living *either* a contemplative life *or* an active life. Author and pastor Eugene Peterson said it like this: "The contemplative life generates and releases an enormous amount of energy into the world— the enlivening energy of God's grace rather than the enervating frenzy of our pride." In its truest form, the contemplative life is not an escape from ministry but the living heart of it.

The contemplative life and the active life are complementary, not either-or. True contemplatives are vibrantly active in the work of the One they contemplate. And those who are truly active in kingdom work live in profound communion with the One with whom they do this work. Contemplation is the root to the tree of holy activity. Contemplation is the inhale to the exhale of godly ministry. Contemplation is the heart of holy leadership, and holy leadership is a fruit of deep-rooted contemplation. If we attempt to make contemplation and action a matter of mutually exclusive choice, our leadership will not be healthy or effective.

THE NATURE OF LEADERSHIP PRAYER

I've sometimes called the sort of prayer I'm talking about here "leadership prayer." How might I distinguish this from other types of prayer? Well, when someone has asked you to pray for them, what kinds of requests have they made? For what did they want you to pray? People ask me to pray for healing, financial concerns, and much-needed jobs. Usually, people hope to see a specific situation changed. How does this compare to how Paul prayed for the churches to whom he wrote? Let's look at his prayer for his brothers and sisters in Thessalonica: "Night and day we pray most earnestly that we may see you again and supply what is lacking in your faith" (1 Thess 3:10). Paul's prayer *focused more on the people's inner life than on their outer life.* His was more soul prayer than situation prayer. I like to think that this is how leaders pray for those they serve.

I want to pray for those I serve like Paul does. I want to focus on soul issues, on spiritual formation issues, on a person's transformational relationship with Jesus! I want to live with—and live out—the realization that central to my leadership is praying that my beloved friends will grow in their relational knowledge of God together (Eph 1:17) and that their love for one another might increase (Phil 1:9). I never want to underestimate the power God releases in people's lives when I hold them in his presence and invite him to enable them to more fully embrace the truth of his great love for them and to then share that love with others freely and generously (Eph 3:16-19).

Leadership prayer is *staying awake to God's presence* as I seek to serve his kingdom purposes in the world around me. At times a leader's venue will be family—husband or wife, sons and daughters, father and mother. Too many times my closest relationships have been lived on unholy autopilot. She does this; you say that. You say that; he does this. We become unthinking, unreflective, unresponsive to one another; our hearts fall asleep. Likewise, my leadership can lag when my heart and mind are lulled to sleep by unreviewed habits. Praying for others keeps my heart awake and alert in my roles and relationships of influence. So *leadership prayer is rooted in love, and love is fully awake.*

Consider now another prayer of Paul for his friends in Thessalonica:

> Now may our God and Father himself and our Lord Jesus clear the way for us to come to you. May the Lord make your love increase and overflow for each other and for everyone else, just as ours does for you. May he strengthen your hearts so that you will be blameless and holy in the presence of our God and Father when our Lord Jesus comes with all his holy ones. (1 Thess 3:11-13)

Paul did pray that God would work circumstances together so that he and his colleagues would be able to return to this young faith community at some point. That prayer is a little situational, but it is mostly Paul's expression of his hope that he might further serve them in their newfound faith. Paul prayed with hope that they would have their hearts strengthened in the presence of God. He wanted them to be beyond full of love for brothers and sisters in Jesus as well as for everyone else in their lives. Paul prayed soul prayers. May we as leaders pray soul prayers so that those we serve might find grace that empowers, encourages, stimulates, and energizes them for every good thing God gives them to do.

In this way, *prayer is more relational than transactional.* There have been times, though, when I assumed that the important thing when I prayed was getting something to happen in a person's life that might have little to do with that person's heart. We could envision intercession as an opportunity to commune and interact with God about people who matter to us, who bother us, who interest us. Intercession is a conversational relationship with God for the benefit of others in our life.

Leadership prayer is also *more person-focused than program-focused.* Too often, though, I've focused my prayer on asking God to bless with success some meeting, service, gathering, service project, or initiative. That's fine as far as it goes, but ultimately I am to be seeking to serve the actual people who attend these events I plan. It has made such a difference when I've focused my prayers on particular people I hope or expect to see at an event. I pray for people whom I believe will be present when I preach a sermon or teach a lesson. Praying for people feels very much like a kingdom activity. Then, when we finally gather, I have eyes to see what kingdom good might be possible.

Finally, leadership prayer aims to *be more God-focused than me-focused*. Perhaps that sounds like an odd thing to say. Isn't prayer, by definition, my saying something to God, asking something of him? Isn't prayer God-oriented in its very essence? I suppose that's true, but my prayers can sometimes become more focused on my worries than on seeking my faithful and trustworthy heavenly Father. Prayer has sometimes become only a self-centered admission of my shortcomings, line crossings, and failures without an honest entering into the presence of one who delights to show mercy (Mic 7:18) and longs to be gracious (Is 30:18). My requests can become half-hearted, self-deprecating hopes rather than humble, confident requests of a more-than-generous Father. Prayer is a reminder that I am not serving myself in ministry, but I am serving a heavenly King who chose me to do the work I do. I've been invited into a valued place in the King's plan and purposes. In prayer I remember this fact and reorient myself to this reality. What an honor!

And what a difference it makes in my heart and my leadership when my prayers are more soul-focused than situation-focused, more relationship-focused than transaction-focused, more people-focused than program-focused, and more God-focused than me-focused!

Approaching God for others is blessed kingdom work that I regard as learning to be in communion with God on behalf of those I care about. I think of Paul's counsel that we "pray in the Spirit on all occasions with all kinds of prayers and requests. With this in mind, be alert and always keep on praying for all the Lord's people" (Eph 6:18). We learn to join, moment by moment, with the intercession of God's Spirit who is continually praying for us in harmony with the purposes of God for us (Rom 8:26-27). When my prayer for others shrinks to some weird perpetual Christmas wish list, I find prayer wearying—a clear indication that I'm praying from a posture of non-abiding. Rather than talking with God from a position of connection with him, I'm launching my requests off toward a God who seems at quite a distance from me.

DYING TO SELF IN PRAYER

Leadership prayer is not merely expressing what I want as I sit in God's presence; instead, it is often a kind of dying to what I *think* I want. This element of prayer is really more about our own spiritual formation than it is about improving any ministry situation. If all of us approached prayer as the practice of dying to ourselves and becoming more alive to God, we would see a majority of our personal struggles with prayer in a very different light. Another aspect of this dying to self is to ask ourselves, "Who in me is praying at this exact moment?" So often, it hasn't really been the true me. God has made the person who is praying, but some mask or persona or voice I think God expects to hear from me is speaking to him. So many of our prayers—especially those we pray at the beginning of our spiritual journeys—are self-centered. We want things from God. We want to feel better, have more, see problems solved, be more important, and so on. As we awaken to God's presence with us, our focus during prayer might, thankfully, move from a crass seeking of outward pleasures to a God-honoring seeking after inward character. We taste delight in God's presence and realize we want more of that. We might even assume that the rich experience of the divine presence is proof positive that we're already well on our way to dying to what is old within us. We might assume that these new feelings of closeness to God are evidence of profound transformation within us. But it's just as possible that we've simply transferred our self-centered orientation from worldly pleasures to divine ones.

I've come to discover that my struggle in prayer tends to correspond to the degree that I am seeking to establish my identity through things I do and through what others say about me. This me is what Brennan Manning, in his book *Abba's Child*, called the impostor, and this impostor often tries to take responsibility (and credit) for my leadership roles. Manning explained it this way:

> Obviously, the impostor is antsy in prayer. He hungers for excitement, craves some mood-altering experience. He is depressed when deprived of the spotlight. The false self is frustrated because he never hears God's voice. He cannot, since God sees no one there. Prayer is death to every identity that does not come from God. The false self flees silence and solitude because they remind him of death.

I become resistant to regular prayer when the impostor operates as primary identity because I don't have my primary identity rooted in something real and God-given. If I am awake enough, I realize that my level of resistance to prayer is a sort of warning light on the dashboard of my leadership, making me aware of this misplaced sense of identity.

We may be mistaken if we assume that experiencing certain spiritual pleasures in prayer is evidence of our spiritual maturity. Much in all of us still needs to die. And as that happens, that old part of us can become attached to spiritual pleasures in place of physical ones. I think this is why God has sometimes withheld the pleasure of his presence or his felt blessing. Such spiritual pleasure might have become for me a means of nourishing something old in me rather than energizing the new person I am in Jesus.

SEASONS WITH GOD

It can be disturbing when the honeymoon-like joys and passions of feeling God's presence with us fade through no apparent fault or wrongdoing on our part. Where we once felt unconquerable and confident in our faith, we may begin to feel less certain. But what if these spiritual delights of youthful faith leave us not as a punishment but as a way of opening up space for something less dramatic and exciting but more substantial and sustainable? What if God is making room for a deep, calm peace, a sense of perfect rest in him? Those first gifts are withdrawn so that we might gain the self-knowledge that we were clinging to the gifts more than we were to God the giver. The continuance of those honeymoon emotions would not have served us well on the longer journey. They were like the first fruits of spring—an exciting new experience that must fade so that the calm, sunlit beauty of summer can replace it.

As we go on, we find that this new and peaceful stillness—our ability to rest in the Lord—has a charm all its own. It is just as joyful as the initial joy but richer in quality. We take great pleasure sinking into its depths! We acknowledge how good it has been to experience a more sober and reflective season since awakening more fully to the everlasting arms. We feel a deeper sense of satisfaction, a growing fullness of our hearts, like a deep pool filling with calm water. Appreciating that "in quietness and confidence is your strength" (Is 30:15 NLT), we may feel as if we have finally let go of self.

But our attachment to this pure and simple peace of God can be too much about ourselves: we might find we're more focused on the peace of God than on the God of peace. And we never become fully aware of how deep this self-love runs until God begins to uproot it out of our hearts—a gardening job that we are utterly unable to perform on ourselves. When the digging begins, we find this deep sense of peace departing, and our journey with God takes us into a parched and lonely wilderness. Our heart feels uninspired and cold, our spiritual feelings are numbed, words of prayer don't come easily, our mind is distracted, and our spirit feels faint. We don't know what to do or how to respond to the arid season. Our self-confidence evaporates: "Why is my conversation with God so different? Did I do something?" Any sense of personal resourcefulness fades, and we feel powerless. God seems to have left the building, and we are left lonely and abandoned.

At this point so many followers of Jesus are tempted to give up on the journey of prayer. Earlier, this temptation grew out of mere human mood. Now we feel tempted because we see no good way forward. We recognize and feel the reality of our nakedness, weakness, waywardness, and deadness apart from God's presence. We realize we will find no rest in our old ways of thinking, choosing, and living. Furthermore, God seems more distant than before we began to trust him. Yet this moment that seems so empty is actually the moment of our salvation, the moment when God is actually surrounding us with the purifying and healing presence of love. The cloud that seems to block God's presence is actually the shadow of God's hand. The abyss of emptiness that gapes within us is a promise of a greater fullness than we can imagine. If we feel we are being diminished, it is only so that we might be all the more enlarged. God withdraws his felt presence from us, reminding us of the simple reality that without him, we really can't do a thing that matters. God desires to enlarge our heart's capacity for love and holy longing, enabling us to receive the fuller revelation of himself that he longs to impart. If we are willing to walk through the wilderness of these spiritually dry and dark seasons with patience and humility, if we offer our dull and empty heart to God in a simple response of love, we will experience the wonders that God works in those desert legs of our journey.

Such spiritual transformation—the result of sustained prayer—has a powerful impact on the work of spiritual leadership. So many of the self-centered motivations that inspired us, motivated us, even drove us begin to fade—and of course this change can be disorienting and disturbing. In fact, as we begin this new way of being, we might be tempted to say that praying has taken the edge off of our leadership.

But what if that edge was not a holy thing after all? We might just discover that it is possible to be compelled by the love of God rather than be driven by less noble, more self-serving motives.

Let me close this chapter in a way that I hope is fitting—with a prayer.

Jesus, thank you for the gifts of my many relationships and roles where I can—by your grace—influence people to follow you more wholeheartedly. Forgive me for those times when I have engaged in those relationships more for my personal benefit than for your kingdom good. Thank you for your patient and persistent work within me as I learn to live my life in prayerful companionship with God. Thank you for enabling me to see my friends, my work, my life from a holier, truer vantage point. Continue your transforming work in me, that I might become the person you created me to be so that you can use me to bless people for their good and your great glory. Amen.

PRACTICE: *INTENTIONAL PRAYER*

I've taken a number of different approaches to organizing my prayer for others over the years. At some point, I've kept a well-organized portfolio of the various groups of people in my life and prayed for them daily, weekly, or monthly. At other times, I've simply set aside time and trusted God's Spirit to bring to mind and heart those I might remember prayerfully in his presence.

At this point in your journey, in what direction are you drawn? Do you want to be more structured and focused in the way you pray for others? Or do you want to set regular time to pray but to be more spontaneous and Spirit-nudged in who you pray for?

If you're drawn in the direction of structure, you might get yourself a binder or journal in which to write down the names of people in your life. You could begin at the relational epicenter with family and close friends, continuing in later pages to list people in your neighborhood, school, church, workplace. When you set aside time to pray, you could pray regularly (i.e., daily) for those closer in and pray weekly for those whose path you cross less frequently. However you structure your prayer for others, pray with a heart and mind that remains in a listening posture. Trust that God's Spirit, who is always praying for these people in your life, might breathe a creative or strategic idea in your mind to help you pray in keeping with the Father's heart.

If you are drawn instead to a more flexible and free approach to praying for others, it can help to set aside some specific amount of time. I sometimes set a gentle timer on my smartphone to help me concentrate on praying and resist the temptation to check the time as I go. Take a few moments first to be silent. Listen. Ask God's Spirit to bring to mind those you might serve in prayer. A word or an idea might come to mind as you think about them. Offer that word up as a word of acknowledgment to God. Say their name aloud in God's presence with a heart trusting that God knows exactly what this person needs right now. Let yourself enter into the reality that God is already involved in their lives in good and beautiful ways. Join him prayerfully in this.

Unhurried Leadership Reflections

1. In this season of your life, how would you describe the relationship between praying and leading? In what ways are they vital and organic in their connection? In what ways do they seem more disconnected and separate? How do you feel about that? How would you like to talk with God about your desires for growth or change?

2. What do you think about the idea that prayer is a means of influence? In what ways does that feel inviting to you? In what ways do you resist such an idea? Let this become a place of conversation with God for a few minutes.

3. Thomas Merton said that "in prayer we discover what we already have." Sometimes prayer is seen as a way of getting something

we don't yet have. In what ways are these two approaches opposed to each other? In what ways might these approaches simply be two sides of the same coin?

4. Set aside ten minutes to pray for people in your life. Ask God's Spirit to help you discern what's on his heart and mind for them. Be slow to speak. Begin with listening. Resist jumping quickly into some of your autopilot liturgies in terms of how you usually pray. Be expectant that God will do something creative and beautiful through you as you bring these friends into God's presence with you.

TEN

Working with God

WHEN I THINK ABOUT MY OWN JOURNEY as a pastor and now as a spiritual director and leader to other leaders and organizations, there are times my activities as a Christian leader were vaguely intended for God, but they didn't spring from God, they weren't inspired by God, and I was not operating with God. I was far more aware of the work I was doing and far less aware of the work God had already been doing and had called me to be a part of. I'm grateful for spiritual mentors who served me and blessed me, teaching me the qualities of a leader who walks with Jesus and works with him (see Mt 11:28-30 *The Message*).

I wonder if a leader who is working with Jesus might somehow become aware of the plans of God's Spirit like Solomon did when he built the temple: "[David] gave [Solomon] the plans of all that the Spirit had put in his mind for the courts of the temple of the LORD and all the surrounding rooms, for the treasuries of the temple of God and for the treasuries for the dedicated things" (1 Chron 28:12). The chronicler goes on to lay out line after line of instructions for layout, interior design, staffing, items to be used in services, and so on. The instructions are quite specific.

Now I'm not expecting what Dallas Willard called a sort of "message a minute" experience of hearing specific assignments from God like divine dictation, but I do think that God's Spirit would enjoy providing us wisdom, creativity, guidance, and empowerment in our day-to-day work.

You have heard the terms *work with God* and *doing God's work.* When I talk about doing God's work, I'm talking about those people who have a formal and perhaps paid leadership position as well as those Jesus-followers who serve without a paycheck from the church and who take initiative without having an official position. The term *working with God* is pretty self-explanatory, but what does that look like in real-life, day-to-day terms? And what is the connection between being in relationship with God and doing God's work?

CONNECTING PRAYER AND LEADERSHIP

To begin, one way to reflect on how working with God actually works is to think in terms of how prayer (relationship with God) and leadership (doing God's work) relate to one another. I see three ways this has worked (or not worked) in my own journey.

First, let's acknowledge that some leaders see the connection more as pray *or* lead rather than pray *and* lead. Perhaps they see themselves as driven extroverts who just don't have the temperament to sit around "doing nothing" in prayer. They are glad that God has put others in the body of Christ, perhaps more introverted than they are, to handle the praying. Of course these busy leaders affirm the importance of prayer—at least in theory—but their practice can be irregular and thin. They see no vital relationship between praying and leading, so they and their communities suffer.

Other leaders see the connection as pray, *then* lead. Regardless of their temperament, these leaders realize that they must have a healthy relationship with God if they are to do his work well. So they cultivate a rhythm of meaningful and life-giving spiritual disciplines in their personal life. But somehow, when it comes time to lead, they consider prayer as just about the last strategy to try. They might open a critical leadership meeting with a few moments of prayer, but prayer gets practically left behind when it comes time for discussion, strategizing, planning, and, later, engaging in the work.

What has worked best for me is an orientation toward pray *and* lead. Consider these benefits: we learn to lead prayerfully, and we learn to pray with an eye for initiative and engagement. I'm suggesting a way of praying and leading in which these activities intersect and interplay rather than being separate and disconnected. We need not see prayer as falling in the "being close to God" category and leadership as falling under the "doing for God at a practical distance" category.

Prayer is living in vital friendship with God. Leadership is working in vital friendship with God.

WORKING WITH GOD: SCRIPTURE

In his letter to the Colossians, Paul wrote, "Whatever you do, whether in word or deed, do it all in the name of the Lord Jesus, giving thanks to God the Father through him" (Col 3:17). What exactly does this look like? Do I close each piece of work or each conversation the way I might close a formal prayer: "In the name of Jesus, amen"? That might be a meaningful thing to do, but more is being said here. Paul is encouraging the followers of Jesus in Colossae—and us along with them—to say what we say and do what we do under the loving authority of Jesus. His is an authority, a lordship that has drawn near to us. It is not authority at a distance. I do not relate to his authority as I might respond to a letter from the IRS or a jury summons. The authority of Jesus is personal and relational. He has invited me to walk with him and work with him.

This piece of counsel appears in the wider context of Colossians 3:12-17 where Paul is helping us see the whole of our lives as seasoned with the character of Jesus, led by the example of Jesus, energized by the presence of Jesus, and sustained by the peace of Jesus. Rather than being a tagline for our words and our work, our choice to act and speak "in the name of Jesus" serves as a vital link to Jesus who walks with us, works with us, dwells among us, and dwells within us. We best speak with others, connect with them, and do our work from such a place of rich intimacy where we are immersed in his presence.

So, here's a practical application. As I draft this chapter, I am doing it as an expression of my communion with God through Jesus. I am not writing these words *for* Jesus so much as I am seeking to write them *with* Jesus. The same can be true about any of our conversations, tasks, or projects. Whatever work is in our schedule today, we can do it *with* Jesus. We can do that work from a posture of gratitude, just as Paul said, "giving thanks to God the Father through [Jesus]" (Col 3:17).

Think about the counsel of James in his letter:

> Now listen, you who say, "Today or tomorrow we will go to this or that city, spend a year there, carry on business and make money." Why, you do not even know what will happen tomorrow. What is your life? You are a mist that appears for a little while and then vanishes. Instead, you ought to say, "If it is the Lord's will, we will live and do this or that." (Jas 4:13-15)

James seems to be reminding us that we can plan all we want for the future, but there is no guarantee that we'll even be here to carry out our plans. Some mistake this as counsel to give up the idea of any kind of planning. I think a better way to approach this is to listen well to James's punch line: we ought to say, "If the Lord wills it, we will do this or that in the future." Again, we need to hear this as a "with God" piece of counsel. We can apply that counsel by engaging in practices that help us discern the heart of God so that our planning will be more rooted in his ways, counsel, and guidance.

Too often, when we begin to plan some future event or engagement, we start with the question "What are we going to do?" It's a reasonable question, but it's not the best *first* question. Perhaps James would have us first ask questions like "What might be on the heart and mind of God in this moment, in this setting, and for these people?" or "In what ways might this opportunity provide just what these people need at this time?" Questions like these, prayerfully asked, provide profound wisdom, rich creativity, and clearer focus as I make my plans.

The apostle Paul also wrote a passage of Scripture that has become a meaningful way of thinking about doing our work with God: "We always thank God for all of you and continually mention you in our prayers. We remember before our God and Father your work produced by faith, your labor prompted by love, and your endurance inspired by hope in our Lord Jesus Christ" (1 Thess 1:2-3). Here Paul told these fellow believers about his continual conversation with God, focused specifically on their work, their labor, and their endurance.

Paul talked about his deep and continual gratitude to God for their friendship and partnership as colaborers. Such gratitude is a response to grace. In fact, I find that gratitude keeps fresh my awareness of just how graced my life and my work really are. Gratitude is a holy engine for further good work we will do in partnership with God. There are always reasons to be thankful. (As a person who can sometimes focus on the cup half empty, I find this statement a good reminder for me.) Gratitude acknowledges the reality of God's grace at work in me and in others. And Paul spoke of offering this gratitude to God in prayer. We continually mention people in our prayers because we care about them, and we realize God cares about them even more than we do. What God does for those we love will last—so we pray.

FAITH, HOPE, LOVE—AND WORK

Think about any work you do to support yourself and your family. You might call it your job or your career. What role does gratitude play in that arena? When you receive your paycheck, for example, is your first thought, *What a generous thing it is to have been given this paycheck!* Probably not. What would you feel if someone expected a "thank you" each time you received a paycheck? Wouldn't you think, "Wait a minute! I *earned* this." Of course you did, but it wouldn't make much sense to say, "You're so nice to give me this paycheck that I earned."

But now think about the underlying grace. God makes us *able* to do the work we do. He opened doors of opportunity for us to do this work, and we can be grateful to God for that grace. And through that work God graciously provides for us by—among other blessings—meeting our very practical needs. (Those blessings include the privilege to work since God created us to work. That work is always an opportunity for us to glorify God, to act as his light in this world, and often to share the truth of the gospel.) So, in our work, we can see much evidence of God's grace and gracious provision, and we can respond to this divine generosity with heartfelt gratitude. When sharing his thoughts about work with the people of Thessalonica, Paul used three phrases that led me to do some important reflecting: "your work *produced by* faith, your labor *prompted by* love, and your endurance *inspired by* hope" (1 Thess 1:3).

Paul first spoke of work being rooted in faith. Dallas Willard defined faith as "confidence grounded in reality." We can work from a place of security, trusting in God's actual presence with us and provision for us. We can do our work with great confidence that God's hand is already fruitfully at work in what he has us doing. Put differently, Jesus would do my job very well, and he is glad to be doing it with me.

This approach is very different from when my work has been fueled by anxiety. That work operates under such assumptions as I will not have what I need to do my work, or my efforts will fall short of my hopes, or something will block my efforts and prevent the good work I wish to do. Anxiety's assumptions have a way of narrowing my vision and dampening my energy and creativity. While anxiety has some-times driven me to a lot of activity, anxiety is not a fruit of the Spirit. So anxiety does not result in *good* work. Faith says, "I work because I believe God is already working." Do you believe this about your current work? Do you believe God is already at work for the good in whatever good work we do in the context of our home, our neigh-borhood, our church ministry, or our job?

Paul also spoke of labor prompted by love. Such work blesses others, helps others, serves others. Labor prompted by self-interest or greed serves only one's own good, one's own kingdom. When self-interest drives us, we have little sense, if any, of doing our work with God. We might welcome God's blessing as long as it corresponds to what we want to have happen, but that's not nearly the same as "your kingdom come, your will be done."

Finally, Paul described an endurance inspired by hope. Hope looks forward and anticipates the unseen but certain goodness that God has for us in that future. We do not do our work alone, but in the presence of the good God who is for us. So hope says, "Thank you, Father, that we get to do this work together." This inspired endurance is so different from dogged, resigned, gritted-teeth endurance that is not fueled by hope.

So when we work *with* God, we work in a way that grows out of and therefore reflects our Christian faith, hope, and love; our work is not a picture of anxiety, despair, or self-serving. We work because God is already working. We don't work assuming God is distant and unin-volved. We work confident that God loves us before we lift a finger: we don't work to *earn* God's love. We hang in there because we know that God's kingdom is a good and safe place to live life and because our future is utterly hope-filled. We can learn to do our work in the presence of a faithful, loving, good God. We can hear God's voice calling us "beloved," so we work *from* love rather than *for* love.

Too many times, though, on a very practical level, I've done work without God. Of course I can't actually do anything without God, but

I'm talking about the sort of practical atheism that has too often characterized seasons of my work. None of us sets out to be atheists in our work, but our sense of God being with us as we work can grow thin. Our heads are down and we're getting things done, but we have little sense of the heart or hand of God with us as we're doing them.

And since many of us spend the majority of our waking hours doing some form of work—chores around the house, personal tasks, schoolwork, work for our job, ministry work—we may be living a large part of our lives without much sense of God's presence. This isn't what we want, but it happens.

At the end of the chapter you will find a simple but powerful practice that has helped many leaders, including me, to sense that we truly are doing our work with God. It begins by listing out everything you do in a week and then reflecting on what it would mean to do those things "with God." I remember doing this exercise with a group of pastors and ministry leaders alongside education and business leaders. As we walked through the steps, I noticed a busy businessman among us checking his pulse after he had written his list. I didn't think much of it, but after he wrote "with God" after all his work items, he was checking his pulse again. I had to ask him what was going on. He said, "When I wrote down my long list of work, I felt my pulse going up. When I took my pulse, it was about twenty beats above normal. When I began to write 'with God' after each item, I felt my pulse go back down. When I checked it, it was back to normal."

BRINGING IT ALL TOGETHER

So, working with God does not begin with the question, What are we going to do? but rather with questions like What is on God's heart? and What would best serve the people? The first question is unintentionally self-focused. The other two questions are more God-centered and people-focused, and that is what working with

God looks like. A simple framework we could use to envision this working-with-God life involves four movements: contemplation, discernment, engagement, and reflection. I've touched some of these themes in this book, but here I'd like to bring them together.

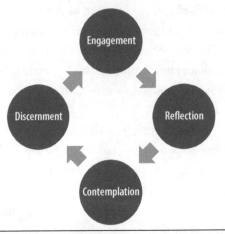

Figure 1. Four movements of working with God

Contemplation. If I were to use the metaphor of a journey to explain this way of working with God moment to moment and day to day, contemplation would represent that we walk with God as our traveling companion in the whole of our life and in all our work. Contemplation is not just a meditative practice. It is personal communion with God. Contemplation is a way of living and working in his presence. A contemplative life is an attentive life in a distracted world. It is a listening life in a wordy world. It is an abiding life in a detached world. It is an unhurried life in a frenetic world.

Contemplation seeks first God's kingdom and his righteousness, not as a theoretical affirmation but as a lived and practiced reality. Contemplation is an orientation to life in which God is first, last, and everything. Contemplation enables us to do our work with a growing and sustaining vision of God with us. Contemplation works in the presence of the King and experiences the reality that all is truly well in his kingdom.

Consider this insight from spiritual director and teacher Thomas Green about how contemplation relates to our work:

> The apostolic life is the overflow of the contemplative. One goes first to the chapel, as it were, to be filled with God, and then goes to the marketplace to share with others the God he has encountered in prayer.

In my metaphor, we walk with God and we work with God, experiencing and expressing God's presence all along the way.

Contemplation is sometimes experienced as a holy conversation. But I must admit that I've sometimes felt intimidated by the practice of intercessory prayer. I felt that others were perhaps more gifted, or I imagined that whatever I would ask for on another's behalf would be far less than what God intended for him or her. I have also been put off by the way I've seen some people practice it: they seemed too intense, too focused on predetermined outcomes, or too wordy.

I have been helped by imagining intercessory prayer in terms of relationship. I think about what it would be like if I could overhear what the Father and the Son are talking about when they talk about the person for whom I am praying. I'm not claiming to have some perfect pipeline to the heavenly realms, but this has been a creative and life-giving way for me to think about intercession.

I think in particular of these verses from Hebrews 7:

> Now there have been many of those priests, since death prevented them from continuing in office; but because Jesus lives forever, he has a permanent priesthood. Therefore he is able to save completely those who come to God through him, because he always lives to intercede for them. (vv. 23-25)

It's that last phrase that captures me: Jesus "always lives to intercede for them." His is a continual, vital, and personal conversation with the Father for my good and for your good. And it seems to me that since Jesus has called me one of his friends (Jn 15:15), he might enjoy interacting with me about his care for people in my life whom—on his behalf—I'd like to bless, serve, influence for his kingdom purposes.

On this theme of contemplation, let me speak briefly to the resistance to and even rejection of contemplation by some of my conservative Christian friends. They feel that any form of contemplation or mysticism is outside the boundaries of orthodox Christian faith. I find such a view puzzling. I see contemplation or even mysticism as experiencing the reality of our biblical understanding of and faith in God revealed in Christ. Contemplation is living in the reality of our theology and doctrine.

Evangelicals have rightly focused on the necessity of believers having a personal relationship with God through Christ. This was the invitation to which I responded as a high school student attending a concert by a jazz group whose lyrics hinted at their own faith in Jesus. I enjoyed the peace, the joy, the sense of belonging that came from entering into this relationship with Jesus in a vital and real way. I experienced God in a living, joyful way, and I see that moment as my first experience of contemplation. A God I had heard a bit about became a God I encountered in reality through Jesus. I don't see contemplation as an esoteric practice that lies outside the framework or tradition of the Christian community over the centuries. It is not separate from the truth of the Scriptures or the truth about God as Christians have framed it in theological terms over the centuries.

And I am not talking about any kind of weird or obscure contemplation that fails to honor the shared biblical convictions about God, his will, and his ways that have been faithfully entrusted to us through the generations. I am talking about a way of actually *living* this relationship with God rather than merely *believing* true statements about such a relationship or just becoming an expert in the doctrines of the broader Christian community or my smaller community within it. I don't want to be a person who honors God with my lips, but whose heart is far from him. As a Christian leader, I don't want to recommend a relationship to others that I am not tending well myself. But I have too often been just that person. I am familiar with the security or confidence that comes with knowing *about* God and talking *about* God that isn't the same as my own actual communion *with* God. The contemplative movement of the journey is staying in close communion with our traveling companion.

Discernment. The second element of this journey of working with God is discernment. In our metaphor of a journey, discernment is the lantern that lights the path just ahead. Discernment is the ability to recognize the light of God's presence shining on the path before me so I can make my way safely and fruitfully. If contemplation is a life in which the prayer of Jesus is answered—"I in them and you in me—so that they may be brought to complete unity" (Jn 17:23)—then discernment is the insight, the wisdom, the ability to see my way forward that is a reflection of that increasingly intimate friendship. Discernment is learning to see God's guiding, even transforming presence in my thoughts, my desires, and my intentions.

One means of discernment is engaging God in reading and reflecting on Scriptures. Doing so will shed greater light on the path before us. Think of those beautiful and familiar words of Psalm 119:105, "Your word is a lamp for my feet, a light on my path." As I allow the light of God's message to shine in my thinking, my heart, my intentions, they are sometimes affirmed and sometimes exposed and then re-formed. Discernment will not usually provide me with a detailed punch list for my day, but it will allow me to see those things I've intended to do in light of God's mind and heart. Discernment may also open my eyes to a piece of work I hadn't anticipated.

Discernment enables us to see God through the eyes of other people. Our vision of God is not individualistic, but communal. We learn to make our way with a greater sensitivity to the hopes and needs of other people. This is not a solitary journey, but a journey in community. Discernment shows us how we might live as servants rather than demanding to be served. On the other hand, discernment also enables us to see people through the eyes of God. We also learn to see God's good and beautiful intentions for others and to work with him toward those ends. We learn to see people not just from an outward perspective, but to discern their hearts.

Engagement. In our metaphor, engagement is simply walking the path of our life and our work. It is practicing the presence of God not just as a spiritual discipline but as a principle for doing the work he has given us to do. When I've thought about practicing the presence of God as Brother Lawrence or Frank Laubach practiced it, I have tended to think of it in terms of a personal spiritual discipline—a Jesus-and-me practice. But what a fruitful opportunity it is to practice God's presence in my life and in my work. I can walk with Jesus and work with Jesus in the unforced rhythms of his life, in the unforced rhythms of his grace for me (see Mt 11:29 *The Message*). I can practice the presence of our Father in heaven who is always working (Jn 5:17). I can engage my work from a place of holy willingness rather than unholy willfulness. A prayer from a recent service at my Anglican church helps me: "Help us to enter their world in love. Help us to experience, with grace, their point of view."

What does engaging our work look like when it is birthed in contemplation and guided by discernment? I find the ideas represented in the acronym *process* a helpful answer to that question: our working with God is **p**rayerful, **r**ooted, **o**rganic, **c**lear, **e**legant, **s**table, and **s**imple. Let me explain.

Prayerful. Holy engagement in our work begins and ends in prayer, and prayerful contemplation is the spirit of the entire journey. Our work can truly be a rich *contemplative* activity.

Rooted. Holy engagement in our work is a journey grounded and rooted in the Scriptures and in the solid traditions of God's people from centuries past. While we must be aware of the unique needs of our times as we work, we can work in the same humble, selfless, gracious, good, honest spirit that Jesus did two thousand years ago. Such work resists the temptation to be captured by the latest leadership fad.

Organic. Holy engagement in our work remains spiritually alive. Jesus uses organic and natural images to describe our connection with him: a sheep with its shepherd, a branch connected to a vine. Such work is relational rather than individualistic: we work with God, and we work with others. It's too easy for our work to become mechanistic, predictable, surprise-resistant, or mystery-eliminating when we work independent of God and his Spirit.

Clear. Holy engagement in our work seeks a simplicity and clarity of purpose. Jesus used straightforward stories to capture people's imaginations and teach profound truths. We do our work with clarity born of divine purpose rather than complexity born of random human will. Rather than working from the mixed motive of self-promotion, we learn to do our work in a way that resists the temptation to be indispensable.

Elegant. Holy engagement in our work reflects the elegant beauty and grace evident in the rest of creation. Elegant work reflects the glorious kingdom of God that gives it birth. We realize that we are working with a divine artist. We are never more creative than when we are working with the Creator.

Stable. Holy engagement in our work with God enables us to work with continuity and perseverance, to be stable and reliable. There is a way of working with God today that works as well now as it did a decade ago, a century ago, a millennium ago. The Scriptures enable us to walk good and ancient paths (Jer 6:16). Christian practices like examen, *lectio divina*, contemplative prayer, and others have endured for centuries. Is what I'm doing now based on God's timeless values as much as it might be?

Simple. Holy engagement in our work finds a way toward simplicity. That's not to say our work is easy. It probably isn't. But we have a way of adding unnecessary complexity to the work that we do. Working with God might enable us to prune certain activities away from our work that aren't fruitful, for example. This is a sort of Occam's Razor test for the work we do.

Reflection. Finally, on this journey toward a life characterized by working with God, we come to reflection, that look back with God over the path we've traveled so far—today, this past week, this past month, however long we choose. Reflection is taking time to learn from the journey so far; it is the spiritual practice of examen. We learn to look back and notice the ways God's grace has attended our path. We acknowledge those moments when we welcomed grace as well as those when we resisted grace. We see when we ran ahead of our traveling companion, when we fell behind, and when we veered off the path altogether. We then acknowledge the mercy and grace that welcome us back to his path of life.

This image of a journey draws a prayer up from within me: *Good Shepherd, you do good work. Enable me to grow as a person who lives my life and does all my work from a place of deep rootedness in you. May I remember that I am never alone even when I feel alone. And when my work provokes fear, may your love overwhelm that fear. When I'm tempted to anxiety, may I relax in the reality that you are with me. Shine your light on the decisions before me. Enable me to choose that which would be life for me and for those with whom I work. I want to learn to walk with you. Teach me how to do my work with you—in you. And teach me to look back with you so that I might learn from that which was fruitful as well as that which was harmful. I want to be an unhurried leader wherever my life and my work take me. In the name of Jesus, amen.*

PRACTICE: *WORKING WITH GOD*

To do this reflection exercise, locate an empty page in your journal or an empty document on your computer to do some writing. Here are the steps you can take to engage this practice:

First, list all your work in a typical week—personal tasks, household chores, job responsibilities, upcoming or regular meetings and appointments, elements of your job description, whatever. Be as thorough as you like.

Next, review your list and ask yourself, *How do I feel about this list?* Write those feeling words below your list. What positive feelings arise? What negative feelings surface? Does this list force you to feel this way? If so, how? If not, why not? Write your reflections.

Now take a few minutes to return to your list of work items and, at the end of each item, write the words "with God" or "with Jesus." Do this slowly and thoughtfully. Don't rush through this step.

How did adding those two little words to each item affect your feelings about these work items? Do you feel the same? Do you feel different? Write words that describe your feelings now.

Take a moment and talk with God about what you learned as well as about what you might do differently in your work as a result of what this little exercise revealed. You could, for example, actually write "with God" next to a calendared appointment or an item on your to-do list.

Unhurried Leadership Reflections

1. At the opening of this chapter, I talked about how prayer relates to leadership. When has this connection been "pray *or* lead" for you, when prayer was fairly detached from leadership? What happens in you when prayer and leadership become disconnected? When have you experienced a more "pray, *then* lead" pattern in your work and leadership? What fruit did this produce, good or bad? Finally, when have you chosen the integrated "pray *and* lead" approach to your ministry responsibilities? What fruit did that bear?

2. We talked about a sort of practical atheism that can sometimes happen in our work. At what moments in your day or week does this tend to become your reality? What do you think Jesus is inviting you to do to become more aware of his presence with you in those very moments? Ask him for wisdom and creativity here.

3. Reflect on Paul's description of the Thessalonians' efforts when he talks about "[their] work produced by faith, [their] labor prompted by love, and [their] endurance inspired by hope" (1 Thess 1:3). In what ways do you experience faith, hope, or love as the motor of your work? In what ways do you recognize your work being instead moved by worry, despair, or self-interest?

Acknowledgments

AT THE END OF PAUL'S MONUMENTAL LETTER to the
church at Rome, he closes with a sort of acknowledgments page. In
it, he mentions twenty-nine individuals in Rome and nine who are
with him as he writes, as well as four groups of Christ-followers. It's
a chapter that some are tempted to skim through because it seems to
lack substantial theology or teaching material.

But this is inspired Scripture. Paul acknowledges these people, most
of whom we would not even know if they weren't mentioned here in
his letter, because *people matter.* They are fellow workers. They are dear
friends. They are mothers and brothers and sisters. Let me mention a
few brothers and sisters, friends and fellow workers, who have been
with me in this writing journey.

I'm grateful for some quiet and beautiful places to write that friends
made available to me along the way: Mike Yearley's home in Simi Valley;
Christ the King Retreat Center in Citrus Heights; Chad and Krista
Wallace's hilltop hacienda in Jarabacoa, Dominican Republic; Doug
Ayres's Paso Robles vineyard guest house; Gary Moon and the Martin
Institute/Dallas Willard Center house at Westmont College in Santa
Barbara (which involved another wonderful train and bicycle journey).

I'm deeply grateful to Lisa Guest for the gift of her review and substantial feedback on early drafts of these chapters. The team at Inter-
Varsity Press has been, as always, a delight. Thank you especially to Cindy
Bunch and Jeff Crosby. This book is far better because of your counsel
and encouragement. I take full responsibility for any shortcomings.

In the midst of this writing project, Gem and I launched a new nonprofit, Unhurried Living. I'm grateful for our board members Tom and Marla, Dave and Cathy, and Danny, as well as our advisory board members Scott, Don, Jeff, Mary, Darrell, and Jeb, for their encouragement, prayers, and support. I'm grateful, too, for a group of about forty friends who prayed regularly for this project. It wouldn't have been nearly as good (or nearly as finished!) without your prayerful help. Finally, thank you to so many financial partners who have donated in support of our work training leaders. Our work, and this book, would be impossible without you.

Finally, I am grateful for my wife, Gem, and three adult sons, Sean, Bryan, and Christopher. What a gift it is to have such a warm and welcoming home in which to do so much of this writing work. You inspire deep joy and great pride in me.

Notes

CHAPTER 1: BECOMING AN UNHURRIED LEADER

11 *the one who hurries:* This is a paraphrased line from Vincent de Paul, a seventeenth-century French priest who was dedicated to serving the poor.

21 *ruthlessly eliminate hurry:* John Ortberg, *The Life You've Always Wanted* (Grand Rapids: Zondervan, 2002), 76.

CHAPTER 2: LEADING FROM ABUNDANCE

30 *The [one] who is wise:* From Bernard of Clairvaux's eighteenth sermon on the Song of Songs. Available online at https://archive.org/stream /StBernardsCommentaryOnTheSongOfSongs/StBernardOnTheSong OfSongsall_djvu.txt. Accessed August 12, 2016.

37 *In religious circles:* Douglas V. Steere, *Dimensions of Prayer* (New York: Women's Division of Christian Service, 1962), 4.

38 *Soul Room and Leadership Room:* Chuck Miller, *The Spiritual Formation of Leaders* (Maitland, FL: Zulon Press, 2007). Miller introduces this image on pp. 11-13, but refers to it throughout much of the book.

40 *Now out from such a holy Center:* Thomas Kelly, *A Testament of Devotion* (San Francisco: HarperSanFrancisco, 1992), 77.

CHAPTER 3: LEADING IN HIS PRESENCE

47 *Jarabacoa in the Dominican Republic:* Thank you, Chad and Krista.

52 *[conspiring] to get [people] involved in anything:* Eugene Peterson, *Christ Plays in Ten Thousand Places* (Grand Rapids: Eerdmans, 2005), 118.

what is most personal: Henri Nouwen, *With Open Hands* (Notre Dame, IN: Ave Maria Press, 1972), 7.

CHAPTER 4: VISION OF GOD, VISION FROM GOD

62 *We Western peoples:* Thomas Kelly, *A Testament of Devotion* (New York: Harper & Brothers, 1941), 70-71.

68 *Every God-given vision:* Oswald Chambers, "Visions Becoming Reality," reading for July 6, 2016, available at http://utmost.org/visions -becoming-reality. Accessed on August 12, 2016.

70 *one-third rule:* In *An Unhurried Life* (Downers Grove, IL: InterVarsity Press, 2013), 170-72, I talked about my friend Paul Jensen's idea of a one-third rule in which, in any leadership training process, one-third of the time is devoted to the actual practice of spiritual, communal, or missional skills.

73 *We do our work for Jesus:* Quoted in Leighton Ford, *The Attentive Life* (Downers Grove, IL: InterVarsity Press, 2008), 132.

CHAPTER 5: QUESTIONS THAT UNHURRY LEADERS

86 *suffering is the greatest teacher:* Baron Friedrich von Hügel, *Letters to a Niece* (London: J. M. Dent & Sons, 1928), xv-xvi.

87 *If we are Christians:* Ibid., xix.

CHAPTER 6: UNHURRIED INFLUENCE

95 *The image involves a pitcher:* The cover image of Chuck Miller's book *The Spiritual Formation of Leaders* (Maitland, FL: Xulon Press, 2007) illustrates this pitcher, cup, saucer, and plate metaphor. You can read his unpacking of it on page 97.

101 *unhurried time with God:* I discuss this discipline in greater detail in *An Unhurried Life* (Downers Grove, IL: InterVarsity Press, 2013), 162-70.

CHAPTER 7: HOW GRACE EMPOWERS LEADERSHIP

112 *Should you be favored with visions:* C. H. Spurgeon, "A Wafer of Honey," *Spurgeon's Expository Encyclopedia* (Grand Rapids: Baker, 1978), 8:289, quoted in Bruce Demarest, *Satisfy Your Soul* (Colorado Springs: NavPress, 1999), 273.

114 *In my desert of despondency:* Tommy Barnett and others, *The Desert Experience* (Nashville: Thomas Nelson, 2001), 42.

116 *make humility your foundation stone:* Jean-Pierre de Caussade, *Self-Abandonment to Divine Providence* (Rockford, IL: Tan Books, 1959), 279.

120   *Being unknown, dying, disciplined:* David Bosch, *Spirituality of the Road* (Eugene, OR: Wipf & Stock, 2001), 76-77.

CHAPTER 8: UNHURRYING OUR THOUGHTS

124   *If we think we are our thoughts:* Martin Laird, *Into the Silent Land* (New York: Oxford University Press, 2006), 77.

127   *eight deadly thoughts:* Mary Margaret Funk, *Thoughts Matter* (New York: Continuum, 2005), 20-21. Funk suggests that these thoughts progress from the simple to the complex. They run from bodily thoughts to relational thoughts to inner life thoughts.

129   *the key is to move:* Laird, *Into the Silent Land*, 103.

130   *the hail of irrelevant stimuli:* Douglas Steere, *Prayer and Worship* (Richmond, IN: Friends United Press, 1978), 19.

       As soon as I decide: Henri Nouwen, *The Way of the Heart* (New York: Harper & Row, 1981), 18.

131   *our bodies may be at the place of prayer:* Laird, *Into the Silent Land*, 103.

132   *thoughts that are thought about:* Funk, *Thoughts Matter*, 20.

CHAPTER 9: PRAYER AS PRIMARY INFLUENCE

143   *Prayer really is someone we are with:* This is an insight my mentor Chuck Miller has shared with me for years.

144   *I wonder if you have seen:* Baron Friedrich von Hügel, *Letters to a Niece* (London: J. M. Dent, 1928), xxix.

       Without personal prayer: Jerome M. Neufelder and Mary C. Coelho, eds., *Writings on Spiritual Direction* (New York: Seabury, 1982), 89.

145   *You start from where you are:* Martin Laird, *Into the Silent Land* (New York: Oxford University Press, 2006), 53.

147   *The contemplative life generates:* Eugene Peterson, *Under the Unpredictable Plant* (Grand Rapids: Eerdmans, 1992), 114-15.

151   *prayer as the practice of dying to ourselves:* What follows is deeply informed by the remarkable insights of E. Herman in her book *Creative Prayer* (London: James Clarke, 1921), 114-17.

152   *the impostor is antsy in prayer:* Brennan Manning, *Abba's Child* (Colorado Springs: NavPress, 1994), 39-40.

CHAPTER 10: WORKING WITH GOD

163 *confidence grounded in reality:* See www.dwillard.org/resources/willard words.asp. Accessed November 10, 2016.

167 *The apostolic life:* Thomas H. Green, *Come Down, Zacchaeus: Spirituality and the Laity* (Notre Dame, IN: Ave Maria Press, 1988), 45.

 unhurried**living**

Many leaders feel hurried, and hurry is costing them more than they realize. Unhurried Living, founded by Alan and Gem Fadling, provides resources and training to help people learn to lead from fullness rather than leading on empty.

Great leadership begins on the inside, in your soul. Learning healthy patterns of rest and work can transform your leadership—your daily influence.

Built on more than twenty-five years of experience at the intersection of spiritual formation and leadership development, Unhurried Living seeks to inspire Christian leaders around the world to rest deeper so they can live fuller and lead better.

We seek to respond to questions many are asking:

Rest deeper: Why do I so often feel more drained than energized? Can I find space for my soul to breathe?

Live fuller: I have tried to fill my life with achievements, possessions, and notoriety, and I feel emptier than ever. Where can I find fullness that lasts?

Lead better: How can I step off the treadmill of mere busyness and make real, meaningful progress in my life and work?

Our purpose is to resource busy people so they can rediscover the genius of Jesus' unhurried way of life and leadership. We do this by . . .

Living all that we are learning so we share with others from experience and wisdom.

Developing digital, print, and video content that encourages the practices of an unhurried life.

Training people in Jesus' unhurried way of living and leading.

Come visit us at unhurriedliving.com to discover free resources to help you

Rest deeper. Live fuller. Lead better.

Web: unhurriedliving.com
Facebook: facebook.com/unhurriedliving
Twitter: @UnhurriedLiving
Instagram: UnhurriedLiving
Email: info@unhurriedliving.com

Also by Alan Fadling

An Unhurried Life
978-0-8308-3573-7

formatio
TRADITION. EXPERIENCE.
TRANSFORMATION.

Formatio books from InterVarsity Press follow the rich tradition of the church in the journey of spiritual formation. These books are not merely about being informed, but about being transformed by Christ and conformed to his image. Formatio stands in InterVarsity Press's evangelical publishing tradition by integrating God's Word with spiritual practice and by prompting readers to move from inward change to outward witness. InterVarsity Press uses the chambered nautilus for Formatio, a symbol of spiritual formation because of its continual spiral journey outward as it moves from its center. We believe that each of us is made with a deep desire to be in God's presence. Formatio books help us to fulfill our deepest desires and to become our true selves in light of God's grace.